First edition January 2013

Published by Design Community College Inc,

Design Community College Inc.
PO Box 1153
Topanga CA 90290 USA

info@curedale.com
Designed and illustrated by Robert Curedale

ISBN-10: 0988236265
ISBN-13: 978-0-9882362-6-4

Structured Workshops
The author presents workshops online and in person in global locations for executives, engineers, designers, technology professionals and anyone interested in learning and applying these proven innovation methods. For information contact: info@curedale.com

50 Selected Design Methods

to transform your design

Robert Curedale

Dedication

Dedicated to aidan, liam, ashton and clayton

introduction

The methods described in this book have been selected by the author from two previously published volumes on design methods which outline 400 design methods. They are appropriate for application across design disciplines.

The methods can be applied by designers and professionals working in design teams in all areas of design and architecture. These are tools to support a trend in most areas of design towards a methods based approach.

The trend is a necessary evolution in the way that design is being done for the many situations in which traditional design skills are not adequate to find the best solution to a design problem. These methods are becoming required skills for designers everywhere. The methods described have been tested and successfully applied across disciplines, across cultures, across the globe. They will enable you to design products, systems buildings, interfaces and experiences with confidence that you have created the most informed design solutions for real people that is possible. We believe that this is the largest collection of design methods that is available and with the companion volume two is an indispensable resource for anyone practicing design.

Traditional design methods equip designers to design the aesthetic qualities of objects, graphics and other physical or digital expressions of design. Designers today are being asked to design these things as integral parts of more complex systems of services and experiences.

These methods allow a designer to balance both analytical and creative thinking processes concurrently and to work effectively as a member of a cross disciplinary design team.

The structure of Western economies has changed over the last five decades. There has been a steady increase in employment in the service sector and a steady decrease of employment in manufacturing as technologies such as robotics replaced labor in factories. In the United States the service sector now employs 90% of the working population. This has risen from around 50% in 1960. Organizations that employ designers need to create design that balances the requirements of complex ecosystems of products, environments, services and experiences both physical and virtual. Traditional design skills such as drawing are effective ways of communicating three dimensional forms and two dimensional graphic design but are not able to describe the forth dimension necessary in service and experience design which is time. Services and experiences change over time.

Traditional design education has cast a designer as a type of artist who essentially works alone and places personal self expression above all else. The methods stress design as a collaborative activity where designers respect and have empathy for the other development team members and where design is informed by an understanding of the perspectives of the people who will eventually use the finished design.

The methods allow a designer to create informed design with logical justifications for their decisions that can be communicated convincingly to managers, engineers and financial people. I have kept the descriptions simple to give readers the essential information to adapt, combine and apply the methods in their own way. I hope that you will gradually build a personal toolkit of favored methods that you have tried and found effective. Different design practitioners can select different methods for their toolkit and apply them in different ways. There is no best combination.

contents

Chapter 1
Design Thinking

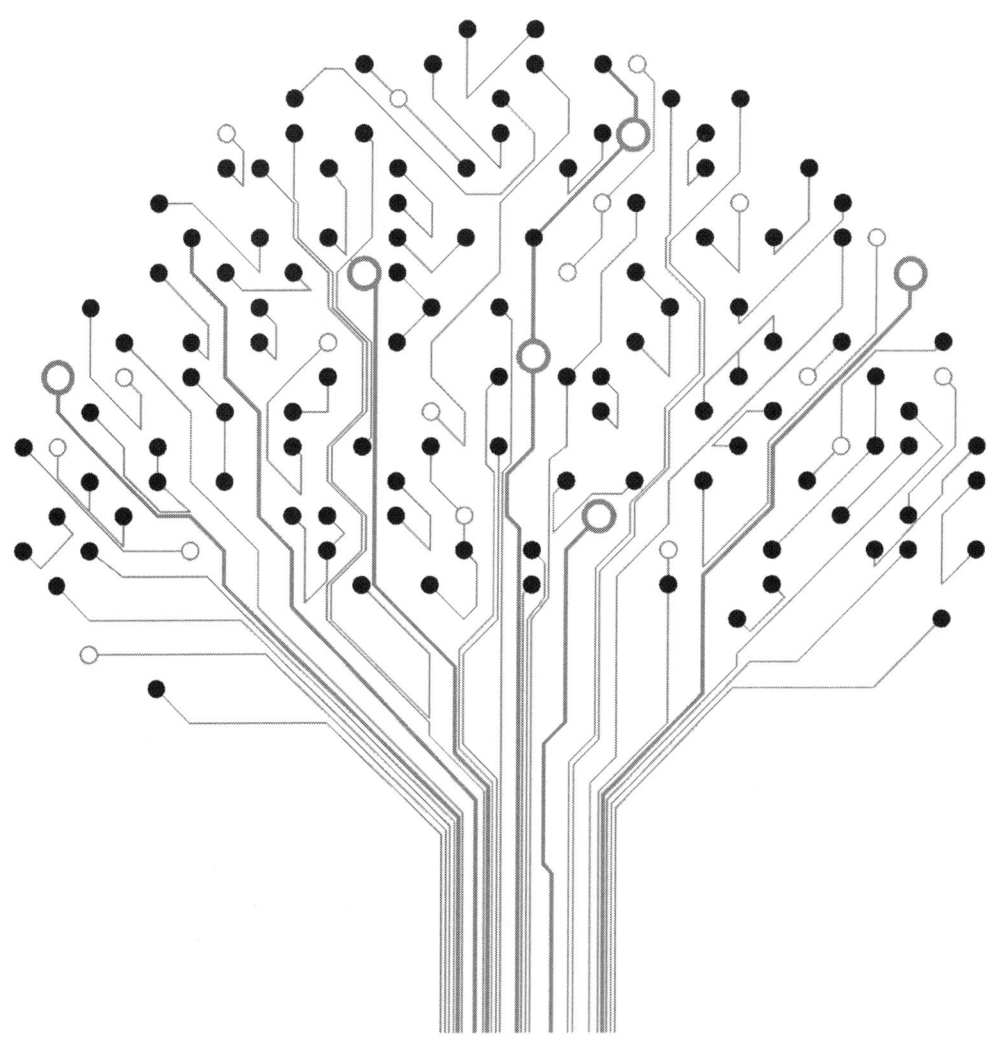

convergent thinking

WHAT IS IT?

Convergent thinking is a tool for problem solving in which the brain is applies a mechanized system or formula to some problem, where the solution is a number of steps from the problem. This kind of thinking is particularly appropriate in science, engineering, maths and technology.

Convergent thinking is opposite from divergent thinking in which a person generates many unique, creative responses to a single question or problem. Divergent thinking is followed by convergent thinking, in which a designer assesses, judges, and strengthens those options. Divergent thinking is what we do when we don't know the answer, when we don't know the next step

WHO INVENTED IT?

Hudson 1967,
Joy Paul Guilford

WHY USE THIS METHOD?

1. Convergent thinking leads to a single best answer, leaving no room for ambiguity.
2. Focuses on recognizing the familiar, reapplying techniques, and accumulating stored information

CHALLENGES

1. Divergent and convergent thinking need to be used together to solve many problems.
2. Designers and business managers are working on many problems which require divergent thinking due to changing complex environments.
3. Traditional management and engineering education stresses convergent thinking.

WHEN TO USE THIS METHOD

1. Explore Concepts
2. Make Plans

HOW TO USE THIS METHOD

Some of the rules of convergent thinking are:

1. Follow a systematic approach, find the patterns affinities and structure in a group of ideas.,
2. Use methods to evaluate ideas, assess qualitative and quantitative measures of ideas,
3. Avoid quickly ruling out an area of consideration, take your time.
4. Do not expend too much time in looking for the optimal solution of an ill-structured multi-criteria problem,
5. Assess risks and have a contingency plan.

REFERENCES

1. Cropley, Arthur (2006). "In Praise of Convergent Thinking". Creativity Research Journal 18: 391—404.

divergent thinking

WHAT IS IT?
The design process is a series of divergent and convergent phases. During the divergent phase of design the designer creates a number of choices. The goal of this approach is to analyze alternative approaches to test for the most stable solution. Divergent thinking is what we do when we don't know the answer, when we don't know the next step. Divergent thinking is followed by convergent thinking, in which a designer assesses, judges, and strengthens those options.

WHO INVENTED IT?
Hudson 1967,
Joy Paul Guilford

WHY USE THIS METHOD?
1. To an extent the number of choices created and compared during the divergent phases of design help determine the quality of the finished design.

CHALLENGES
1. Use when objectives are changing or ill defined.
1. Divergent and convergent thinking need to be used together to solve many problems.
2. Designers and business managers are working on many problems which require divergent thinking due to changing complex environments.

Image Copyright sippakorn, 2012
Used under license from Shutterstock.com

WHEN TO USE THIS METHOD
1. Frame insights
2. Explore Concepts
3. Make Plans

HOW TO USE THIS METHOD
Some of the rules for divergent thinking are:
1. Reframe the problem
2. See the problem from different perspectives,
3. Connect with and have empathy with the people that you are designing for.
4. Defer negative criticism.
5. Generate lots of ideas.
6. Combine and modify ideas,
7. Stretch the ideas, imagine ideas beyond normal limits,
8. Do not be afraid to break paradigms

RESOURCES
1. Pens
2. Paper
3. White board
4. Dry erase markers
5. Post it notes.

REFERENCES
1. Wade, Carole; Tavris, Carol (2008). Invitation to Psychology. Upper Saddle River, NJ: Pearson – Prentice Hall. pp. 258. ISBN 0-13-601609.

design thinking

WHAT IS IT?

Design Thinking is a methodology or approach to designing that should help you be more consistently innovative. It involves methods that enable empathy with people, it focuses on people. It is a collaborative methodology that involves iterative prototyping. It involves a series of divergent and convergent phases. It combines analytical and creative thinking approaches. It involves a toolkit of methods that can be applied to different styles of problems by different types of people. Anyone can use Design Thinking. It can be fun.

WHO INVENTED IT?

The origins of new design methods date back to before the 1950s. 1987 Peter Rowe, Professor at the Harvard Graduate School of Design, published "Design Thinking" the first significant usage of the term "Design Thinking" in literature. After 2000 the term became widely used.

CHALLENGES

1. There has been little research to validate claims about Design Thinking by advocates.
2. Some critics of Design Thinking suggest that it is a successful attempt to brand a set of existing concepts and frameworks with a appealing idea.

WHY USE DESIGN THINKING?

Design Thinking is useful when you have:
1. A poorly defined problem.
2. A lack of information.
3. A changing context or environment
4. It should result in consistently innovative solutions.

Design Thinking seeks a balance of design considerations including:
1. Business.
2. Empathy with people.
3. Application of technologies.
4. Environmental consideration.

Design Thinking seeks to balance two modes of thinking:
1. Analytical thinking
2. Creative Thinking

Advocates of Design Thinking believe that the approach results in consistently innovative design solutions oriented towards people.

Design Thinking takes a cross disciplinary team approach. It rejects the idea of a designer being a lone expert artist working in a studio remote from people in favor of an approach where a designer collaborates with a multidisciplinary team. Design Thinking advocates making informed decisions based on evidence gathered from the people and context in place of designers working on a hunch.

WHEN TO USE DESIGN THINKING

Design Thinking is an approach that can be applied throughout the design process:

1. Define intent
2. Know Context
3. Know User
4. Frame insights
5. Explore Concepts
6. Make Plans
7. Deliver Offering

RESOURCES

1. Paper
2. Pens
3. Camera
4. Notebook
5. Post-it-notes
6. Cardboard
7. White board
8. Dry-erase markers

REFERENCES

1. Martin, Roger L. The Opposable Mind: How Successful Leaders Win through Integrative Thinking. Boston, MA: Harvard Business School, 2007.
2. Buchanan, Richard, "Wicked Problems in Design Thinking," Design Issues, vol. 8, no. 2, Spring 1992
3. Cross, Nigel. "Designerly Ways of Knowing." Design Studies 3.4 (1982): 221-27.
4. Brown, Tim, and Katz, Barry. Change by Design: How Design Thinking Transforms Organizations and Inspires Innovation. New York: Harper Business, 2009.
5. Florida, Richard L. The Rise of the Creative Class: and How It is Transforming Work, Leisure, Community and Everyday Life. New York, NY: Basic, 2002 Basic, 2002
6. Jones, John Christopher. Design Methods. New York: John Wiley & Sons, 1970.

design thinking

FOCUS ON PEOPLE:

Design is more about people than it is about things. It is important to stand in those people's shoes, to see through their eyes, to uncover their stories, to share their worlds. Start each design by identifying a problem that real people are experiencing. Use the methods in this book selectively to gain empathy and understanding. and to inform your design. Good process is not a substitute for talented and skilled people on your design team.

GET PHYSICAL

Make simple physical prototypes of your ideas as early as possible. Constantly test your ideas with people. Do not worry about making prototypes beautiful until you are sure that you have a resolved final design. Use the prototypes to guide and improve your design. Do a lot of low cost prototypes to test how Your Ideas physically work. using cardboard, paper, markers, adhesive tape, photocopies, string and popsicle sticks. The idea is to test your idea, not to look like the final product. Expect to change it again. Limit your costs to ten or twenty dollars. Iterate, test and iterate. Do not make the prototype jewelry. It can stand in the way of finding the best design solution. In the minds of some a high fidelity prototype is a finished design solution rather than a tool for improving a design. You should make your idea physical as soon as possible. Be the first to get your hands dirty by making the idea real.

BE CURIOUS

Ask why? Explore and Experiment. Go outside your comfort zone. Do not assume that you know the answer. Look for inspiration in new ways and places. Christopher Columbus and Albert Einstein followed their curiosity to new places.

SEEK TEAM DIVERSITY

A diverse design team will produce more successful design than a team that lacks diversity. Innovation needs a collision of different ideas and approaches. Your team should have different genders, different ages, be from different cultures, different socioeconomic backgrounds and have different outlooks to be most successful. With diversity expect some conflict. Manage conflict productively and the best ideas will float to the surface. Have team members who have lived in different countries and cultures and with global awareness. Cross cultural life experience enables people to be more creative.

TAKE CONSIDERED RISKS

Taking considered risks is helps create differentiated design. Many designers and organizations do not have the flexibility or courage to create innovative, differentiated design solutions so they create products and services that are like existing products and services and must compete on price.
"It takes a lot of courage to release the familiar and seemingly secure, to embrace the new, but there is no real security in what is no longer meaningful. There is more security in the adventurous and exciting, for in movement there is life, and in change, there is power."
Alan Cohen

USE THE TOOLS

To understand the point of view of diverse peoples and cultures a designer needs to connect with those people and their context. The tools in this book are an effective way of seeing the world through the eyes of those people.

LEARN TO SEE AND HEAR

Reach out to understand people. Interpret what you see and hear. Read between the lines. Make new connections between the things you see and hear.

COMBINE ANALYTICAL AND CREATIVE THINKING

Effective collaboration is part of effective design. Designers work like members of an orchestra. We need to work with managers, engineers, salespeople and other professions. Human diversity and life experience contribute to better design solutions.

LOOK FOR BALANCE

Design Thinking seeks a balance of design factors including:
1. Business.
2. Empathy with people.
3. Application OF technology.
4. Environmental consideration.

TEAM COLLABORATION

Design today is a more complex activity than it was in the past. Business, technology, global cultural issues, environmental considerations, and human considerations all need careful consideration. Design Thinking recognizes the need for designers to be working as members of multidisciplinary multi skilled teams.

The need for creative self expression for designers is important. For an artist the need for creative self expression is a primary need. For a designer this need must be balanced by an awareness and response to the needs of others. Balanced design needs analytical as well as creative thinking. The methods in this book balance a designer's creative thinking with analytical thinking. This balance comes most effectively from a team rather than from an individual. Designers must respond to the needs of the design team, the needs of the business needs of those who employ us to design and the needs of those people that we design for.

design thinking process

DEFINE THE VISION?
What are we looking for?

1. Meet with key stakeholders to set vision
2. Assemble a diverse team
3. Develop intent and vision
4. Explore scenarios of user experience
5. Document user performance requirements
6. Define the group of people you are designing for. What is their gender, age, and income range. Where do they live. What is their culture?
7. Define your scope and constraints
8. Identify a need that you are addressing. Identify a problem that you are solving.
9. Identify opportunities
10. Meet stakeholders

KNOW THE PEOPLE AND CONTEXT
What else is out there?

1. Identify what you know and what you need to know.
2. Document a research plan
3. Benchmark competitive products
4. Create a budgeting and plan.
5. Create tasks and deliverables
6. Explore the context of use
7. Understand the risks
8. Observe and interview individuals, groups, experts.
9. Develop design strategy
10. Undertake qualitative, quantitative, primary and secondary research.
11. Talk to vendors

EXPLORE IDEAS
How is this for starters?

1. Brainstorm
2. Define the most promising ideas
3. Refine the ideas
4. Establish key differentiation of your ideas
5. Investigate existing intellectual property.

PROTOTYPE TEST AND ITERATE
How could we make it better?

1. Make your favored ideas physical.
2. Create low-fidelity prototypes from inexpensive available materials
3. Develop question guides
4. Develop test plan
5. Test prototypes with stakeholders
6. Get feedback from people.
7. Refine the prototypes
8. Test again
9. Build in the feedback
10. Refine again.
11. Continue iteration until design works.
12. Document the process.
13. When you are confident that your idea works make a prototype that looks and works like a production product.

DELIVER
Let's make it. Let's sell it.

1. Create your proposed production design
2. Test and evaluate
3. Review objectives
4. Manufacture your first samples
5. Review first production samples and refine.
6. Launch
7. Obtain user feedback
8. Conduct field studies
9. Define the vision for the next product or service.

Chapter 2
50 Design Methods

Put individual answers or ideas on post-it-notes Spread post-it-notes or cards on a wall or large table.

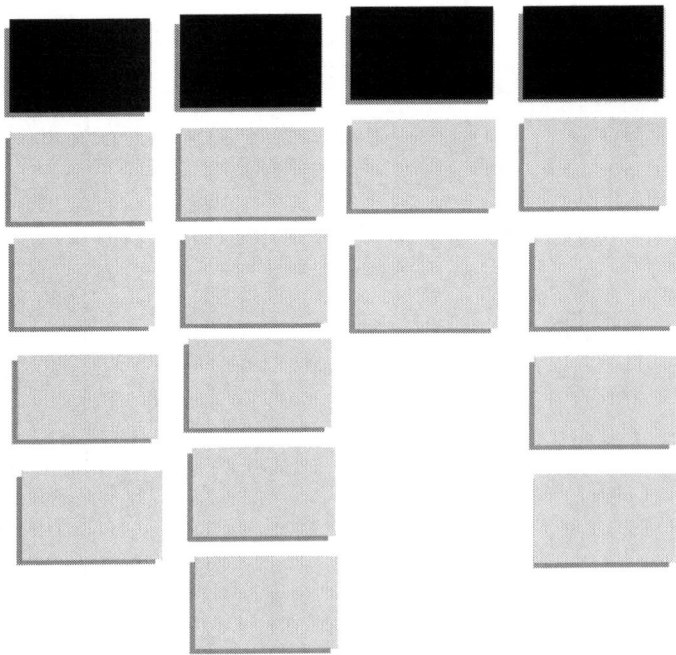

Group similar items and name each group with a different colored card or Post-it-note above the group.

affinity diagram

WHAT IS IT?

Affinity diagrams are a tool for analyzing large amounts of data and discovering relationships which allow a design direction to be established based on the affinities. This method may uncover important hidden relationships.

Affinity diagrams are created through consensus of the design team on how the information should be grouped in logical ways.

WHO INVENTED IT?

Jiro Kawaita, Japan, 1960

WHY USE THIS METHOD?

Traditional design methods are less useful when dealing with complex or chaotic problems with large amounts of data. This method helps to establish relationships of affinities between pieces of information. From these relationships insights and relationships can be determined which are the starting point of design solutions. It is possible using this method to reach consensus faster than many other methods.

RESOURCES

1. White board
2. Large wall spaces or tables
3. Dry-erase markers
4. Sharpies
5. Post-it notes
6. Digital camera

WHEN TO USE THIS METHOD

1. Know Context
2. Know User
3. Frame insights

HOW TO USE THIS METHOD

1. Select your team
2. Place individual opinions or answers to interview questions or design concepts on post-it-notes or cards.
3. Spread post-it-notes or cards on a wall or large table.
4. Group similar items.
5. This can be done silently by your design team moving them around as they each see affinities. Work until your team has consensus.
6. Name each group with a different colored card or Post-it-note above the group.
7. Repeat by grouping groups.
8. Rank the most important groups.
9. Photograph results
10. Analyze affinities and create insights.
11. 5 to 20 participants

REFERENCES

1. Brassard, M. (1989). The Memory Jogger Plus+, pp. 17 - 39. Methuen, MA: Goal/QPC.
2. King, R. (1989). Hoshin Planning, The Developmental Approach, pp. 4-2 - 4-5. Methuen, MA: Goal/QPC.

backcasting

WHAT IS IT?
Backcasting is a method for planning
the actions necessary to reach desired
future goals. This method is often applied
in a workshop format with stakeholders
participating. The future scenarios are
developed for periods of between 1 and 20
years in the future.
The participants first identify their goals and
then work backwards to identify the
necessary actions to reach those goals.

WHO INVENTED IT?
AT&T 1950s, Shel 1970s

WHY USE THIS METHOD?
1.   It is inexpensive and fast
2.   Backcasting is a tool for identifying,
     planning and reaching future goals.
3.   Backcasting provides a strategy to reach
     future goals.

CHALLENGES
1.   Need a good moderator
2.   Needs good preparation

RESOURCES
1.   Post-it-notes
2.   White board
3.   Pens
4.   Dry-erase markers
5.   Cameras

WHEN TO USE THIS METHOD
1.   Define intent
2.   Know Context
3.   Know User
4.   Frame insights
5.   Explore Concepts
6.   Make Plans
7.   Deliver Offering

HOW TO USE THIS METHOD
A typical backcasting question is"How would
you define success for yourself in 2015?
1.   Define a framework
2.   Analyze the present situation in relation
     to the framework
3.   Prepare a vision and a number of desirable
     future scenarios.
4.   Back-casting: Identify the steps to
     achieve this goal.
5.   Further elaboration, detailing
6.   Step by step strategies towards achieving
     the outcomes desired.
7.   Ask do the strategies move us in the right
     direction? Are they flexible strategies?.
     Do the strategies represent a good return
     on investment?
8.   Implementation, policy, organization
     embedding, follow-up

REFERENCES
1.   Quist, J., & Vergragt, P. 2006. Past and
     future of backcasting: The shift to
     stakeholder participation and a proposal
     for a methodological framework. Futures
     Volume 38, Issue 9, November 2006,
     1027-1045

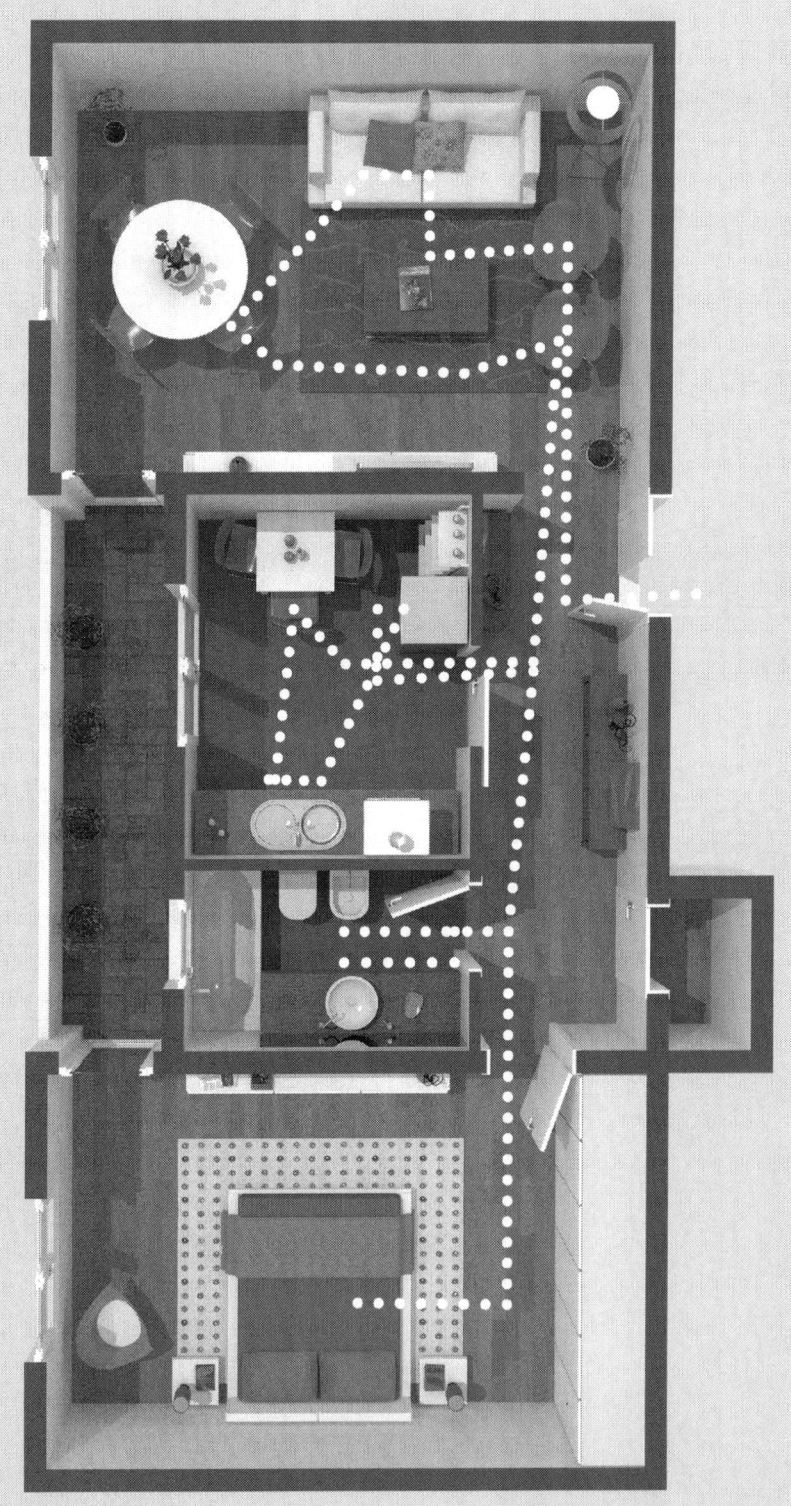

behavioral map

WHAT IS IT?
Behavioral mapping is a method used to record and analyze human activities in a location. This method is used to document what participants are doing and time spent at locations and travelling. Behavioral maps can be created based on a person or a space

WHO INVENTED IT?
Ernest Becker 1962

WHY USE THIS METHOD?
1. This method helps develop an understanding of space layouts, interactions and experiences and behaviors.
2. Helps understand way finding.
3. Helps optimize use of space.
4. A limitation of this method is that motivations remain unknown.
5. Use when you want to develop more efficient or effective use of space in retail environments, exhibits, architecture and interior design.

WHEN TO USE THIS METHOD
1. Define intent
2. Know Context
3. Know User
4. Frame insights
5. Explore Concepts
6.

Image: © Memendesig. | Dreamstime.com

HOW TO USE THIS METHOD
1. Decide who are the users.
2. Ask what is the purpose of the space?
3. Consider what behaviors are meaningful.
4. Consider different personas.
5. Participants can be asked to map their use of a space on a floor plan and can be asked to reveal their motivations.
6. Can use shadowing or video ethnographic techniques.
7. Create behavioral map.
8. Analyze behavioral map
9. Reorganize space based on insights.

RESOURCES
1. A map of the space.
2. Video camera
3. Digital still camera
4. Notebook
5. Pens

REFERENCES
1. Nickerson 1993: Bnet. Understanding your consumers through behavioral mapping.
2. A Practical Guide to Behavioral Research Tools and Techniques. Fifth Edition Robert Sommer and Barbara Sommer ISBN13: 9780195142099ISBN10: 0195142098

   Aug 2001

benjamin franklin method

WHAT IS IT?
A method developed by Benjamin Franklin for making decisions.

WHO INVENTED IT?
Benjamin Franklin 1772

WHY USE THIS METHOD?
1. It is simple
2. It was developed and used by Benjamin Franklin who was a successful decision maker.

WHEN TO USE THIS METHOD
1. Explore Concepts

RESOURCES
1. Pen
2. Paper
3. White board
4. Dry erase markers
5. Post-it-notes

HOW TO USE THIS METHOD
Quote from a letter from Benjamin Franklin to Joseph Priestley London, September 19, 1772

"To get over this, my Way is, to divide half a Sheet of Paper by a Line into two Columns, writing over the one Pro, and over the other Con. Then during three or four Days Consideration I put down under the different Heads short Hints of the different Motives that at different Times occur to me for or against the Measure. When I have thus got them all together in one View, I endeavour to estimate their respective Weights; and where I find two, one on each side, that seem equal, I strike them both out: If I find a Reason pro equal to some two Reasons con, I strike out the three. If I judge some two Reasons con equal to some three Reasons pro, I strike out the five; and thus proceeding I find at length where the Ballance lies; and if after a Day or two of farther Consideration nothing new that is of Importance occurs on either side, I come to a Determination accordingly.

And tho' the Weight of Reasons cannot be taken with the Precision of Algebraic Quantities, yet when each is thus considered separately and comparatively, and the whole lies before me, I think I can judge better, and am less likely to take a rash Step; and in fact I have found great Advantage from this kind of Equation, in what may be called Moral or Prudential Algebra"

bhag

WHAT IS IT?

BHAG stands for Big Hairy Audacious Goal.
It is a type of goal that is bigger than a usual mission statement.

Some examples of BHAGs are:

1. Google bhag is to make all digital information in the world accessible to people everywhere
2. Nokia bhag is to connect one billion people to the internet. For the first time.

WHO INVENTED IT?

J Collins and J Porras,1996

WHY USE THIS METHOD?

1. Bold visions stimulate bold steps
2. BHAGs encourage you to set your sights high and long term.

WHEN TO USE THIS METHOD

Define intent

RESOURCES

1. Pen
2. Paper
3. White board
4. Dry erase markers

HOW TO USE THIS METHOD

1. It needs to motivate people and get them excited.
2. It shouldn't be in your comfort zone
3. It should take a herculean effort to achieve.
4. It should not be possible to achieve with incremental change.
5. BHAGs have time frames of 10-30 years.
6. The BHAG should be aligned to the organization's core values.

REFERENCES

1. Collins, J and Porras, J. Built to Last: Successful Habits of Visionary Companies. Harper Business; 1 edition (November 2, 2004) ISBN-10: 0060566108 ISBN-13: 978-0060566104

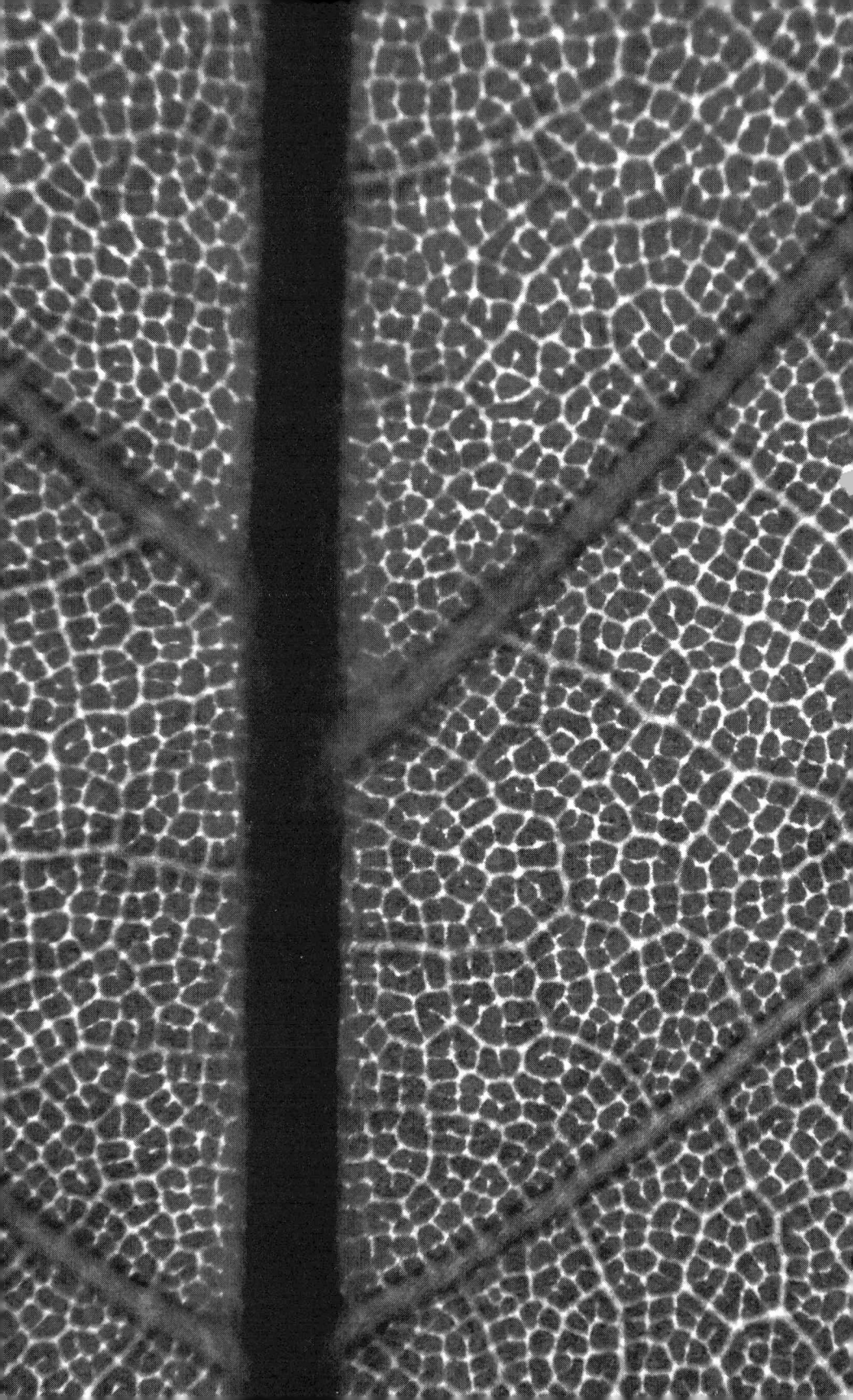

biomimicry

WHAT IS IT?
Biomimicry or biometics is taking inspiration from nature to solve human problems,

WHO INVENTED IT?
Philip Steadman 1979. Popularized by Janine Benyus in her book Biomimicry 1997

WHY USE THIS METHOD?
1. For billions of years nature has evolved and refined living things, systems and materials.
2. Humans have been inspired by nature throughout our existence.
3. Solutions inspired by nature are often better solutions than we can come up with on our own.

CHALLENGES
1. Using a biomimicry may lead you into unknown territory.
2. Our system of business woks independently and sometimes in conflict with nature.

WHEN TO USE THIS METHOD
1. Define intent
2. Know Context
3. Know User
4. Frame insights
5. Explore Concepts
6. Make Plans
7. Deliver Offering

HOW TO USE THIS METHOD
1. Develop the problem
2. Translate the brief into biological parameters.
3. Research natural models that may relate to the design problem.
4. Identify patterns.
5. Create solutions based on nature.
6. Review solutions against natural principles
7. Use nature to stimulate ideas.

RESOURCES
1. Camera
2. Video camera
3. Note pad
4. White board
5. Dry-erase pens

REFERENCES
1. Benyus, Janine (1997). Biomimicry: Innovation Inspired by Nature. New York, NY, USA: William Morrow & Company, Inc. ISBN 978-0-688-16099-9.
2. Hargroves, K. D. & Smith, M. H. (2006). Innovation inspired by nature Biomimicry. Ecos, (129), 27-28.
3. Vogel, S., Cats' Paws and Catapults: Mechanical Worlds of Nature and People. Norton & co. 2000.
4. Pyper, W. (2006). Emulating nature: The rise of industrial ecology. Ecos, (129), 22-26.

Photo: photocase.com – akai

	ACTIVITY PHASE	ACTIVITY PHASE	ACTIVITY PHASE	ACTIVITY PHASE	ACTIVITY PHASE	ACTIVITY PHASE
CUSTOMER ACTIONS	What does user do?					
TOUCHPOINTS	moments places customer contact					
LINE OF INTERACTION						
DIRECT CONTACT	What your Staff do					
LINE OF VISIBILITY						
BACK OFFICE	What your Staff do					
EMOTIONAL EXPERIENCE	+ −					

blueprint

WHAT IS IT?
A blueprint is a process map often used to describe the delivery of services information is presented as a number of parallel rows of activities. These are sometimes called swim lanes. They may document activities over time such as:
1. Customer Actions
2. Touch points
3. Direct Contact visible to customers
4. Invisible back office actions
5. Support Processes
6. Physical Evidence
7. Emotional Experience for customer.

WHO INVENTED IT?
Lynn Shostack 1983

WHEN TO USE THIS METHOD
1. Know Context
2. Know User
3. Frame insights

WHY TO USE THIS METHOD
1. Can be used for design or improvement of existing services or experiences.
2. Is more tangible than intuition.
3. Makes the process of service development more efficient.
4. A common point of reference for stakeholders for planning and discussion.
5. Tool to assess the impact of change.

HOW TO USE THIS METHOD
1. Define the service or experience to focus on.
2. A blueprint can be created in a brainstorming session with stakeholders.
3. Define the customer demographic.
4. See though the customer's eyes.
5. Define the activities and phases of activity under each heading.
6. Link the contact or customer touchpoints to the needed support functions
7. Use post-it-notes on a white board for initial descriptions and rearrange as necessary drawing lines to show the links.
8. Create the blueprint then refine iteratively.

RESOURCES
1. Paper
2. Pens
3. White board
4. Dry-erase markers
5. Camera
6. Blueprint templates
7. Post-it-notes

REFERENCES
1. (1991) G. Hollins, W. Hollins, Total Design: Managing the design process in the service sector, Trans Atlantic Publications
2. (2004) R. Kalakota, M.Robinson, Services Blueprint: Roadmap for Execution, Addison-Wesley, Boston.

brainstorming: nhk method

WHAT IS IT?
The NHK method is a rigorous iterative process of brainstorming of ideas following a predetermined structure.

WHO INVENTED IT?
Hiroshi Takahashi

WHY USE THIS METHOD?
1. This method requires that a quantity of ideas is generated.

CHALLENGES
1. Groupthink
2. Not enough good ideas
3. Taking turns
4. Freeloading
5. Inhibition
6. Lack of critical thinking
7. A group that is too large competes for attention.

WHEN TO USE THIS METHOD
1. Explore Concepts

RESOURCES
1. Paper
2. Pens
3. White board
4. Dry-erase markers
5. Post-it-notes.

HOW TO USE THIS METHOD
1. Define problem statement.
1. Each participant writes down five ideas on five separate cards.
2. Create groups of five participants
3. While each person explains their ideas, the others continue to record new ideas.
4. Collect, and create groups of related concepts.
5. Form new groups of two or three people Brainstorm for half an hour.
6. Groups organize ideas and present them to the larger group.
7. Record all ideas on the white board.
8. Form larger groups of ten people and work further brainstorm each of the ideas on the white board.

REFERENCES
1. Clark , Charles Hutchinson. Brainstorming: The Dynamic New Way to Create Successful Ideas Publisher: Classic Business Bookshelf (November 23, 2010) ISBN-10: 1608425614 ISBN-13: 978-1608425617
2. Rawlinson J. Geoffrey Creative Thinking and Brainstorming. Jaico Publishing House (April 30, 2005) ISBN-10: 8172243480 ISBN-13: 978-8172243487

brainstorming: method 635

WHAT IS IT?

Method 635 is a structured form of brain-storming. "

Here six participant gain a thorough under-standing of the task at hand and them sepa-rately writes three rough ideas for solution. These three ideas are then passed on the one of the other participants who read and add three additional ideas or modifications. This process continues until all participants have expanded or revised all original ideas. Six participants, three ideas, five rounds of supplements" (Löwgren and Stolterman 2004).

WHO INVENTED IT?

Professor Bernd Rohrbach 1968

WHY USE THIS METHOD?

1. Can generate a lot of ideas quickly
2. Participants can build on each others ideas
3. Ideas are recorded by the participants
4. Democratic method.
5. Ideas are contributed privately.

SEE ALSO

1. Brainwriting
2. Dot voting

WHEN TO USE THIS METHOD

1. Frame insights
2. Explore Concepts

HOW TO USE THIS METHOD

1. Your team should sit around a table.
2. Each team member is given a sheet of paper with the design objective written at the top.
3. Each team member is given three minute to generate three ideas.
4. Your participants then pass the sheet of paper to the person sitting on their left.
5. Each participant must come up with thre new ideas.
6. The process can stop when sheets come around the table.
7. Repeat until ideas are exhausted. No discussion at any stage.
8. No discussion.
9. Analyze ideas as a group,

RESOURCES

1. Paper
2. Pens
3. White board
4. Large table

REFERENCES

1. Rohrbach, Bernd: Creativity by rules – Method 635, a new technique for solving problems first published in the German sales magazine "Absatzwirtschaft", Volume 12, 1969. p73-75 and Volume 1 1 October 1969.

brainstorming: related contexts

WHAT IS IT?

A method that involves discovering and projecting the thinking of another sector, brand, organization or context onto a design problem.

WHY USE THIS METHOD?

A method of discovering affinities that can facilitate innovative thinking and solutions.

1. Scenarios become a focus for discussion which helps evaluate and refine concepts.
2. Usability issues can be explored.
3. Scenarios help us create an end to end experience.
4. Personas give us a framework to evaluate possible solutions.

CHALLENGES

1. Strong personalities can influence the group in negative ways.
2. Include problem situations
3. Hard to envision misuse scenarios.

WHEN TO USE THIS METHOD

1. Know Context
2. Know User
3. Frame insights
4. Generate Concepts

HOW TO USE THIS METHOD

1. Identify a design problem
2. Put together a design team of 4 to 12 members with a moderator.
3. Brainstorm a list of sectors, organizations, or contexts that may imply a different approach or thinking to your design problem.
4. Imagine your design problem with the associated list.
5. Generate concepts for each relationship
6. Vote for favored directions using dot voting method.
7. Analyze and summarize insights.

RESOURCES

1. Post-it notes
2. White board
3. Paper
4. Pens
5. Dry-erase markers

REFERENCES

1. "Scenarios," IDEO Method Cards. ISBN 0-9544132-1-0
2. Carroll, John M. Making Use: Scenario-based design of human-computer interactions. MIT Press, 2000.
3. Carroll J. M. Five Reasons for Scenario Based Design. Elsevier Science B. V. 2000.

brainstorming: scamper

WHAT IS IT?
SCAMPER is a brainstorming technique and creativity method that uses seven words as prompts.
1. Substitute.
2. Combine.
3. Adapt.
4. Modify.
5. Put to another use.
6. Eliminate.
7. Reverse.

WHO INVENTED IT?
Bob Eberle based on work by Alex Osborne

WHY USE THIS METHOD?
1. Scamper is a method that can help generate innovative solutions to a problem.
2. Leverages the diverse experiences of a team.
3. Makes group problem solving fun.
4. Helps get buy in from all team members for solution chosen.
5. Helps build team cohesion.
6. Everyone can participate.

CHALLENGES
1. Some ideas that you generate using the tool may be impractical.
2. Best used with other creativity methods

SEE ALSO
1. Brainstorming

WHEN TO USE THIS METHOD
1. Generate concepts

HOW TO USE THIS METHOD
1. Select a product or service to apply the method.
2. Select a diverse design team of 4 to 12 people and a moderator.
3. Ask questions about the product you identified, using the SCAMPER mnemonic to guide you.
4. Create as many ideas as you can.
5. Analyze
6. Prioritize.
7. Select the best single or several ideas to further brainstorm.

RESOURCES
1. Pens
2. Post-it-notes
3. A flip chart
4. White board or wall
5. Refreshments

REFERENCES
1. Scamper: Creative Games and Activities for Imagination Development. Bob Eberle April 1, 1997 ISBN-10: 1882664248 ISBN-13: 978-1882664245

SCAMPER QUESTIONS

SUBSTITUTE

1. What materials or resources can you substitute or swap to improve the product?
2. What other product or process could you substitute?
3. What rules could you use?
4. Can you use this product in another situation?

COMBINE

1. Could you combine this product with another product?
2. Could you combine several goals?
3. Could you combine the use of the product with another use?
4. Could you join resources with someone else?

ADAPT

1. How could you adapt or readjust this product to serve another purpose or use?
2. What else is the product like?
3. What could you imitate to adapt this product?
4. What exists that is like the product?
5. Could the product adapt to another context?

MODIFY

1. How could you change the appearance of the product?
2. What could you change ?
3. What could you focus on to create more return on investment?
4. Could you change part of the product?

PUT TO ANOTHER USE

1. Can you use this product in another situation?
2. Who would find this product useful?
3. How would this product function in a new context?
4. Could you recycle parts of this product to create a new product?

ELIMINATE

1. How could you make the product simpler?
2. What features, parts, could you eliminate?
3. What could you understate or tone down?
4. Could you make the product smaller or more efficient?
5. Would the product function differently if you removed part of the product?

REVERSE

1. What would happen if you changed the operation sequence?
2. What if you do the reverse of what you are trying to do?
3. What components could you substitute to change the order of this product?
4. What roles could you change?

card sort: open

WHAT IS IT?
This is a method for discovering the relationships of a list of items. Participants asked to arrange individual, unsorted items into groups. For an open card sort the user defines the groups rather than the researcher.

Card sorting is applied when:
1. When there is a large number of items.
2. The items are similar and difficult to organize into categories.
3. Users may have different perceptions related to organizing the items.

WHO INVENTED IT?
Jastrow 1886
Nielsen & Sano 1995

WHY USE THIS METHOD?
1. It is a simple method using index cards,
2. Used to provide insights for interface design.

CHALLENGES
1. Ask participants to fill ot a second card if they feel it belongs in two groups.
2. There are a number of online card sorting tools available.

RESOURCES
1. Post cards
2. Pens
3. Post-it-notes
4. Laptop computer
5. A table

WHEN TO USE THIS METHOD
1. Know Context
2. Know User
3. Frame insights
4. Explore Concepts

HOW TO USE THIS METHOD
1. Recruit between 5 and 15 participants representative of your user group.
2. Provide a small deck of cards.
3. Provide clear instructions. Ask your participants to arrange the cards in ways that make sense to them. 100 cards takes about 1 hour to sort.
4. The user sorts labelled cards into groups by that they define themselves.
5. The user can generate more card labels.
6. If users do not understand a card ask them to exclude it. Ask participants for their rationale for any dual placements of cards.
7. Analyze the piles of cards and create a list of insights derived from the card sort.
8. Analyze the data. Proximity or similarity matrixes, dendrograms, and tree diagrams help create a taxonomical hierarchy for the items being grouped

REFERENCES
1. Jakob Nielsen (May 1995). "Card Sorting to Discover the Users' Model of the Information Space".
2. Jakob Nielsen (July 19, 2004). "Card Sorting: How Many Users to Test"

card sort: closed

WHAT IS IT?

This is a method for understanding the relationships of a number of pieces of data. Participants asked to arrange individual, unsorted items into groups. A closed sort involves the cards being sorted into groups where the group headings may be defined by the researcher. There are a number of tools available to perform card sorting activities with survey participants via the internet.

Card sorting is applied when:
1. When there is a large number pieces of data.
2. The individual pieces of data are similar.
3. Participants have different perceptions of the data.

WHO INVENTED IT?

Jastrow 1886

Nielsen & Sano 1995

WHY USE THIS METHOD?

1. It is a simple method using index cards,
2. Used to provide insights for interface design.

CHALLENGES

1. Ask participants to fill out a second card if they feel it belongs in two groups.

REFERENCES

1. Jakob Nielsen (May 1995). "Card Sorting to Discover the Users' Model of the Information Space".
2. Jakob Nielsen (July 19, 2004). "Card Sorting: How Many Users to Test".

WHEN TO USE THIS METHOD

1. Know Context
2. Know User
3. Frame insights
4. Explore Concepts

HOW TO USE THIS METHOD

1. Recruit 15 to 20 participants representative of your user group.
2. Provide a deck of cards using words and or images relevant to your concept.
3. Provide clear instructions. Ask your participants to arrange the cards in ways that make sense to them. 100 cards takes about 1 hour to sort.
4. The user sorts labelled cards into groups by under header cards defined by the researcher.
5. The user can generate more card labels.
6. If users do not understand a card ask them to exclude it. Ask participants for their rationale for any dual placements of cards.
7. Discuss why the cards are placed in a particular pile yields insight into user perceptions.
8. Analyze the data. Create a hierarchy for the information
9. Use post cards or post-it notes.

RESOURCES

1. Post cards
2. Pens
3. Post-it-notes
4. Laptop computer
5. A table

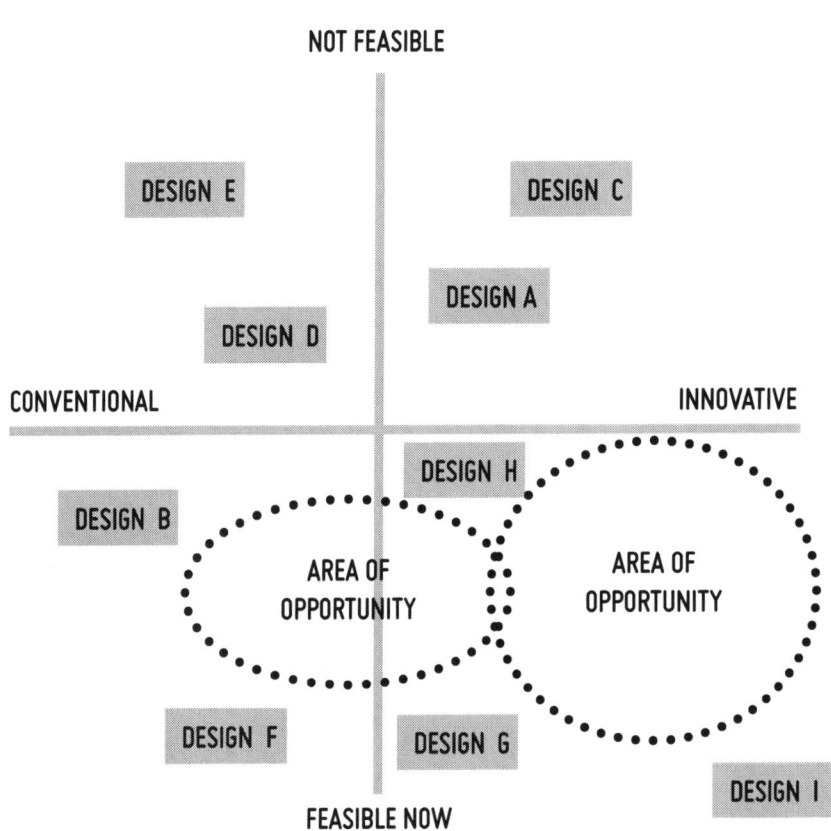

NOT FEASIBLE

DESIGN E

DESIGN C

DESIGN A

DESIGN D

CONVENTIONAL

INNOVATIVE

DESIGN H

DESIGN B

AREA OF
OPPORTUNITY

AREA OF
OPPORTUNITY

DESIGN F

DESIGN G

DESIGN I

FEASIBLE NOW

c-box

WHAT IS IT?

A c-box is a type of perceptual map that allows comparison and evaluation of a large number of ideas generated in a brainstorming session by a design team. The method allows everyone to contribute in a democratic way. It can be used to identify the most feasible and innovative ideas. It is up to your team to decide the level of innovation that they would like to carry forward from the idea generation or divergent phase of the project to the convergent or refinement and implementation phases.

WHO INVENTED IT?

Marc Tassoul, Delft 2009

WHY USE THIS METHOD?

1. It is democratic
2. It is quick and productive
3. It is inexpensive

WHEN TO USE THIS METHOD

1. Frame insights
2. Explore Concepts

REFERENCES

Tassoul, M. (2006) Creative Facilitation: a Delft Approach, Delft: VSSD.

HOW TO USE THIS METHOD

1. The moderator defines the design problem
2. You group can be optimally from 4 to 20 people.
3. On a white board or large sheet of paper create two axes. You can also use tape on a large wall.
4. The team should sit around a table facing the wall.
5. Innovation on the horizontal and feasibility on the vertical axes creating 4 quadrants
6. The scale on the innovation ranges from not innovative at the left hand to highly innovative on the right hand end.
7. Alternative axes are attractiveness and functionality.
8. The scale for feasibility runs from not feasible now at the bottom to immediately feasible at the top.
9. Hand out ten post-it-notes to each member of your team.
10. Brainstorm concepts. Each team member to generate 5 to 10 concepts over 30 minutes. One idea per post-it note. Hand out more post-it notes if required.
11. Concepts can be simple sketches or written ideas or a combination of the two.
12. Each team member then presents each idea taking one to three minutes per idea depending on time available.
13. With the group's input discuss the ideas and precise position on the map.
14. Position each post-it-note according to the group consensus.

CRITICAL SUCCESS FACTOR CHART

FACTOR   BRAND

	A			B			C			D		
	−	+	++	−	+	++	−	+	++	−	+	++
Cost		x			x				x	x		
Brand			x			x	x					x
Technology		x		x				x		x		
Employees	x				x		x				x	
Customer service		x				x			x		x	
Distribution			x	x				x		x		
Speed to market			x			x	x					x
Design		x		x			x				x	
Reliability		x			x				x			x

critical success factor

WHAT IS IT?

The critical success factor is the factor that is necessary for a project to achieve it's goal or mission. In order to be profitable and survive, a company needs to have a critical success factor.

WHO INVENTED IT?

The term success factor was developed by D. Ronald Daniel of McKinsey & Company in 1961. John F. Rockart further developed the concept of critical success factors between 1979 and 1981

WHY USE THIS METHOD?

1. It is a method of graphically representing a company's critical success factors so they can be the focus for discussion and refinement.
2. It is a method of comparing competitors

CHALLENGES

1. The method can be subjective

RESOURCES

1. Pen
2. Paper
3. Computer
4. Graphics software

WHEN TO USE THIS METHOD

1. Define intent

HOW TO USE THIS METHOD

1. Ask your team: 'Why would customers choose us?'."What do we need to do well to win business?" The answer is typically a critical success factor.
2. Create a matrix and rate each identified critical success factor an a 3 point scale.
3. Graph each score and connect the scores for each company being assessed with a line.

REFERENCES

1. Boynlon, A.C., and Zmud, R.W. 1984. "An Assessment of Critical Success Factors," Sloan Management Review (25:4), pp. 17-27.
2. Rockart, John F. "A Primer on Critical Success Factors" published in The Rise of Managerial Computing: The Best of the Center for Information Systems Research, edited with Christine V. Bullen. (Homewood, IL: Dow Jones-Irwin), 1981, OR, McGraw-Hill School Education Group (1986)
3. Johnson, James A. and Michael Friesen (1995). The Success Paradigm: Creating Organizational Effectiveness Through Quality and Strategy New York: Quorum Books. ISBN 978-0-89930-836-4

crowd funding

WHAT IS IT?

Crowdfunding is asking a crowd of people to donate a defined amount of money for a specific cause or project in exchange for various rewards. There are three general categories crowdfunding can fall under: Equity, Donation, and Debt.

1. Equity-based crowdfunding
2. Donation-based crowdfunding
3. Debt-based crowdfunding

WHO INVENTED IT?

In 1997, fans financed a U.S. tour for the British rock group Marillion,

WHY USE THIS METHOD?

1. Relatively low risk for designer and founder.
2. Allows designers to create and make their own products.
3. Fast and efficient.

CHALLENGES

1. Intellectual property protection can be more complicated.
2. Platforms may limit the funds that you can receive.
3. New regulations and tax considerations
4. Clearly articulate what it is you're trying to accomplish in a way that inspires people to want to back it.
5. Define a compelling reward for the members of the crowd.

WHEN TO USE THIS METHOD

1. Deliver Offering

HOW TO USE THIS METHOD

Instructions for Kickstarter.com:

1. A designer visits a site and proposes an idea
2. The community reviews the proposal,
3. The idea is accepted or rejected.
4. The designer launches their project.
5. The designer creates a video to communicate the idea.
6. The designer structures a reward for backers.
7. This is often one of what is being created.
8. In film, dance or theater the reward may be a ticket.

REFERENCES

1. The Geography of Crowdfunding, NET Institute Working Paper No. 10-08, Oct 2010
2. Ordanini, A.; Miceli, L.; Pizzetti, M.; Parasuraman, A. (2011). "Crowd-funding: Transforming customers into investors through innovative service platforms". Journal of Service Management 22 (4): 443.

crowd sourcing

WHAT IS IT?

Crowd sourcing involves out sourcing a task to a dispersed group of people. It usually refers to tasks undertaken by an undefined public group rather than paid employees.

Types of crowd sourcing include:

1. Crowd funding
2. Crowd purchasing
3. Micro work

The incentives for crowd sourcing can include: immediate payoffs, delayed payoffs, and social motivation, skill variety, task identity, task autonomy, direct feedback from the job

WHO INVENTED IT?

Jeff Howe first used the term in a June 2006 Wired magazine article "The Rise of Crowd sourcing"

WHY USE THIS METHOD?

1. Crowd sourcing can obtain large numbers of alternative solutions.
2. It is relatively fast
3. Inexpensive.
4. Diverse solutions.
5. group of people is sometimes more intel-ligent than an individual

CHALLENGES

1. A faulty results caused by targeted, mali-cious work efforts
2. Ethical concerns
3. Difficulties in collaboration and team activity of crowd members.
4. Lack of monetary motivation

WHEN TO USE THIS METHOD

1. Define intent
2. Know Context
3. Know User
4. Frame insights
5. Explore Concepts
6. Make Plans
7. Deliver Offering

HOW TO USE THIS METHOD

1. Define your problem
2. Define your use of the crowd
3. Identify incentives.
4. Identify mechanism to reach the crowd.
5. Inspire your users to create
6. Distribute brief to the crowd
7. Analyze results.
8. Create preferred design solution.
9. Repeat above stages as necessary to refine the design.

RESOURCES

1. A social or other network
2. Crowd sourcing site or interface
3. A mechanism to reach the crowd.
4. An incentive for the crowd.
5. A crowd

REFERENCES

1. Jeff Howe (2006). "The Rise of Crowd sourcing". Wired.
2. Howe, Jeff (2008), "Crowd sourcing: Why the Power of the Crowd is Driving the Future of Business", The International Achievement Institute.

cultural probe

WHAT IS IT?

A cultural probe is a method of collecting information about people, their context and their culture. The aim of this method is to record events, behaviors and interactions in their context. This method involves the participants to record and collect the data themselves.

WHO INVENTED IT?

Bill Gaver Royal College of Art London 1969

WHY USE THIS METHOD?

1. This is a useful method when the participants that are being studied are hard to reach for example if they are travelling.
2. It is a useful technique if the activities being studied take place over an extended period or at irregular intervals.
3. The information collected can be used to build personas.

CHALLENGES

4. It is important with this method to select the participants carefully and give them support during the study.

SEE ALSO

1. Diary study

Image Copyright Tim_Booth , 2013
Used under license from Shutterstock.com

WHEN TO USE THIS METHOD

1. Define intent
2. Know Context
3. Know User
4. Frame insights

HOW TO USE THIS METHOD

1. Define the objective of your study.
2. Recruit your participants.
3. Brief the participants
4. Supply participants with kit. The items in the kit are selected to collect the type of information you want to gather and can include items such as notebooks, diary, camera, voice recorder or post cards.
5. You can use an affinity diagram to analyze the data collected

RESOURCES

1. Diary
2. Notebooks
3. Pens
4. Post-it notes
5. Voice recorder
6. Post cards
7. Digital Camera

REFERENCES

1. Bailey, Kathleen M. (1990) The use of diary studies in teacher education programs In Richards, J. C. & Nunan, D. (org.). Second Language Teacher Education (pp. 215-226). Cambridge: Cambridge University Press.

ANTICIPATE   ENTER   ENGAGE   EXIT   REVIEW

CUSTOMER MORE POSITIVE EXPERIENCES

CUSTOMER POSITIVE EXPERIENCES

BASELINE

CUSTOMER NEGATIVE EXPERIENCES

CUSTOMER MORE NEGATIVE EXPERIENCES

EMOTIONAL EXPERIENCE

customer experience map

WHAT IS IT?

Customer experience also called customer journey mapping is a method of documenting and visualizing the experiences that customers have as they use a product or service and their responses to their experiences.

It allows your team to access and analyze the interacting factors that form a customer experience.

WHY USE THIS METHOD?

1. Helps develop a consistent, predictable customer experience,
2. Presents an overview of your customer's experience from their point of view.
3. Helps reduce the number of dissatisfied customers
4. Can be used with different personas.

WHEN TO USE THIS METHOD

1. Know Context
2. Know User
3. Frame insights

HOW TO USE THIS METHOD

1. Identify your team.
2. Identify the customer experience to be analyzed. Identify the context. Identify personas.
3. Define the experience as a time line with stages such as anticipation, entry, engagement, exit, and reflection.
4. Use post-it notes to add positive and negative experiences to the relevant parts of the time line.
5. Order the experiences around a baseline by how positive or negative the experience were.
6. Analyze the parts of the time line and activities that have the most negative experiences. These are opportunities for design.

RESOURCES

1. Post-it-notes
2. Printed or projected template
3. White board
4. Markers

REFERENCES

1. Joshi, Hetal. "Customer Journey Mapping: The Road to Success." Cognizant. (2009) Web. 26 Jul. 2012.
2. World Class Skills Programme. "Customer Journey Mapping." Developing Responsive Provision. (2006): n. page. Web. 27 Jul. 2012.

day in the life

WHAT IS IT?

A study in which the designer observes the participant in the location and context of their usual activities, observing and recording events to understand the activities from the participant's point of view. This is sometimes repeated. Mapping a 'Day in the Life' as a storyboard can provide a focus for discussion.

WHO INVENTED IT?

ALex Bavelas 1944

WHY USE THIS METHOD?

1. This method informs the design process by observation of real activities and behaviors.
2. This method provides insights with relatively little cost and time.

CHALLENGES

1. Choose the participants carefully
2. Document everything. Something that seems insignificant may become significant later.

WHEN TO USE THIS METHOD

1. Know Context
2. Know User
3. Frame insights

HOW TO USE THIS METHOD

1. Define activities to study
2. Recruit participants
3. Prepare
4. Observe subjects in context.
5. Capture data,
6. Create storyboard with text and timeline.
7. Analyze data
8. Create insights.
9. Identify issues
10. Identify needs
11. Add new/more requirements to concept development

RESOURCES

1. Camera
2. Notebook
3. Video camera
4. Voice recorder
5. Pens

REFERENCES

1. Shadowing: And Other Techniques for Doing Fieldwork in Modern Societies [Paperback] Barbara Czarniawska. Publisher: Copenhagen Business School Pr (December 2007) ISBN-10: 8763002159 ISBN-13: 978-8763002158

design charette

WHAT IS IT?

A design charette is a collaborative design workshop usually held over one day or several days. Charettes are a fast way of generating ideas while involving diverse stakeholders in your decision process. Charettes have many different structures and often involve multiple sessions. The group divides into smaller groups. The smaller groups present to the larger group.

WHO INVENTED IT?

The French word, "charrette" spelt with two r's means "cart" This use of the term is said to originate from the École des Beaux Arts in Paris during the 19th century, where a cart, collected final drawings while students finished their work.

WHY USE THIS METHOD?

1. Fast and inexpensive.
2. Increased probability of implementation.
3. Stakeholders can share information.
4. Promotes trust.

CHALLENGES

1. Managing workflow can be challenging.
2. Stakeholders may have conflicting visions.

WHEN TO USE THIS METHOD

1. Define intent
2. Know context and user
3. Frame insights
4. Explore concepts
5. Make Plans

RESOURCES

1. Large space
2. Tables
3. Chairs
4. White boards
5. Dry-erase markers
6. Camera
7. Post-it-notes

REFERENCES

1. Day, C. (2003). Consensus Design: Socially Inclusive Process. Oxford, UK, and Burlington, MA: Elsevier Science, Architectural Press.

design intent statement

WHAT IS IT?

Designs are created for a purpose. The design intent is a written statement of the creative objectives of the design While not describing the final design solution, the design intent provides the design team with a target for their efforts. It often gives a description of the problem to be sold, information about how the solution will be used.

WHY USE THIS METHOD?

1. A design intent statement provides a focus for design efforts throughout a project.

CHALLENGES

1. The statement of intent should be clear and unambiguous to all team members.

WHEN TO USE THIS METHOD

1. Define intent

HOW TO USE THIS METHOD

1. A design intent statement is best based on an understanding of a particular problem being addressed or a need identified.
2. This can be the result of research such as observation or interviews with the user group.
3. It includes information about the scope of the solution.

QUESTIONS FOR DESIGN INTENT

1. Is the problem clear?
2. Are the objectives clear?
3. Is there agreement on the design intent by all stakeholders?
4. What are the constraints?
5. Have assumptions been tested?
6. What are the risks?
7. What are the business objectives
8. What re the user objectives
9. What are the environmental objectives
10. What are the technology objectives?

Photo: photocase.com – complize

diary study

WHAT IS IT?
This method involves participants recording specific events, feelings or interactions, in a diary supplied by the researcher. User Diaries help provide insight into behavior. Participants record their behavior and thoughts. Diaries can uncover behavior that may not be articulated in an interview or easily visible to outsiders.

WHO INVENTED IT?
Gordon Allport, may have been the first to describe diary studies in 1942.

WHY USE THIS METHOD?
1. Can capture data that is difficult to capture using other methods.
2. Useful when you wish to gather information and minimize your influence on research subjects.
3. When the process or event you're exploring takes place intermittently or
4. When the process or event you're exploring takes place over a long period.

CHALLENGES
1. Process can be expensive and time consuming.
2. Needs participant monitoring.
3. Diary can fit into users' pocket.
4. It is difficult to get materials back.

WHEN TO USE THIS METHOD
1. Know Context
2. Know User
3. Frame insights

HOW TO USE THIS METHOD
1. A diary can be kept over a period of one week or longer.
2. Define focus for the study.
3. Recruit participants carefully.
4. Decide method: preprinted, diary notebook or online.
5. Prepare diary packs. Can be preprinted sheets or blank 20 page notebooks with prepared questions or online web based diary.
6. Brief participants.
7. Distribute diaries directly or by mail.
8. Conduct study. Keep in touch with participants.
9. Conduct debrief interview.
10. Look for insights.

RESOURCES
1. Diary
2. Preprinted diary sheets
3. Online diary
4. Pens
5. Disposable cameras
6. Digital camera
7. Self addressed envelopes

REFERENCES
1. Bailey, Kathleen M. (1990) The use of diary studies in teacher education programs In Richards, J. C. & Nunan, D. (org.). Second Language Teacher Education (pp. 215-226). Cambridge: Cambridge University Press.

SEE ALSO
Empathy probe

disney method

WHAT IS IT?

The Disney method is a parallel thinking technique. It allows a team to discuss an issue from four perspectives. It involves parallel thinking to analyze a problem, generate ideas, evaluate ideas, and to create a strategy. It is a method used in workshops. The four thinking perspectives are – Spectators, Dreamers, Realist's and Critics.

WHO INVENTED IT?

Dilts, 1991

WHY USE THIS METHOD?

1. Allows the group top discuss a problem from four different perspectives

CHALLENGES

1. An alternative to De Bono Six hat Method.
2. Will deliver a workable solution quickly.

WHEN TO USE THIS METHOD

1. Explore Concepts

HOW TO USE THIS METHOD

1. At the end of each of the four sessions the participants leave the room and then at a later time reenter the room then assuming the personas and perspectives of the next group. Time taken is often 60 to 90 minutes in total.
2. The spectator's view. Puts the problem in an external context. How would a consultant, a customer or an outside observer view the problem?
3. The Dreamers view. Looking for an ideal solution. What would our dream solution for this be? What if? Unconstrained brainstorm. Defer judgement. Divergent thinking. What do we desire? If we could have unlimited resources what would we do? They list their ideas on the white board.
4. Realists view. The realists are convergent thinkers. How can we turn the dreamer's views into reality? Looking for ideas that are feasible, profitable, customer focused and can be implemented within 18 months. They look through the dreamer's ideas on the white board and narrow them down to a short list, discuss them and choose the single best idea and create an implementation plan. What steps are necessary to implement this idea? Who can approve it, how much funding is needed? They draw the plan on the whiteboard and then leave the room.
5. The Critics view. What are the risks and obstacles? Who would oppose this plan? What could go wrong? Refine, improve or reject. Be constructive. This group defines the risks and obstacles, make some suggestions and write down these ideas on the white board.

RESOURCES

1. White board
2. Dry erase markers.
3. Pens
4. Post-it-notes.
5. A private room

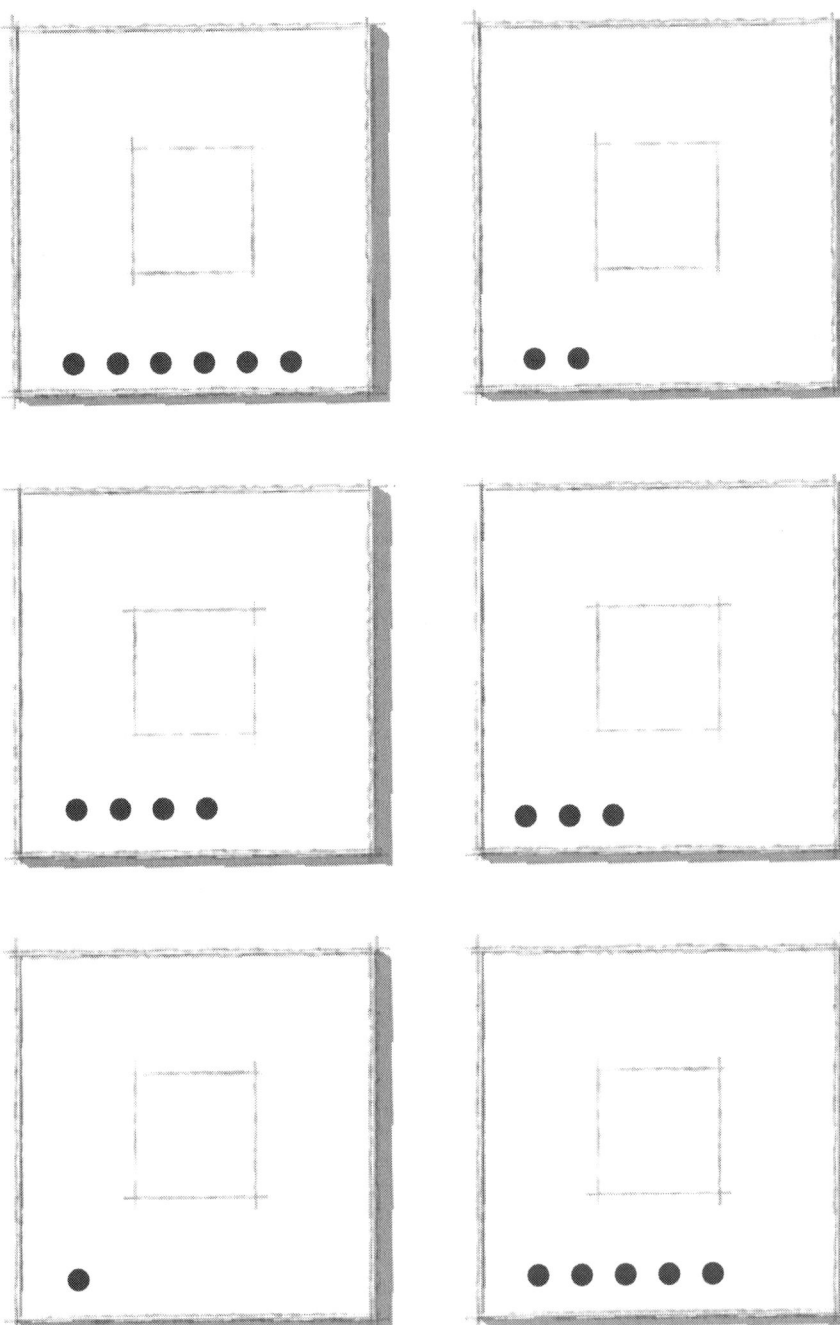

dot voting

WHAT IS IT?

This method is a collective way of prioritizing and converging on a design solution that uses group wisdom. Concepts can be individually scored against selection criteria such as the business proposition, ease of manufacturing, cost and usability. Each participant scores each concept against a list of assessment criteria and the scores are totaled to determine the favored ideas.

WHY USE THIS METHOD?

It is a method of selecting a favored idea by collective rather than individual judgment. It is a fast method that allows a design to progress. It leverages the strengths of diverse team member viewpoints and experiences.

CHALLENGES

1. The assessment is subjective.
2. Groupthink
3. Not enough good ideas
4. Inhibition
5. Lack of critical thinking

RESOURCES

1. Large wall
2. Adhesive dots

REFERENCES

1. Dotmocracy handbook Jason Diceman Version 2.2 March 2010 ISBN 45152708X EAN-13 9781451527087

WHEN TO USE THIS METHOD

1. Define intent
2. Know Context
3. Know User
4. Frame insights
5. Explore Concepts
6. Make Plans
7. Deliver Offering

HOW TO USE THIS METHOD

1. Select a team of between 4 and 20 cross disciplinary participants.
2. Brainstorm ideas for example ask each team member to generate six ideas as sketches.
3. Each idea should be presented on one post it note or page.
4. Each designer should quickly explain each idea to the group before the group votes.
5. Spread the ideas over a wall or table.
6. Ask the team to group the ideas by similarity or affinity.
7. Ask the team to vote on their two or three favorite ideas and total the votes. You can use sticky dots or colored pins to indicate a vote or a moderator can tally the scores.
8. Rearrange the ideas so that the ideas with the dots are grouped together, ranked from most dots to least.
9. Talk about the ideas that received the most votes and see if there is a general level of comfort with taking one or more of those ideas to the next step.

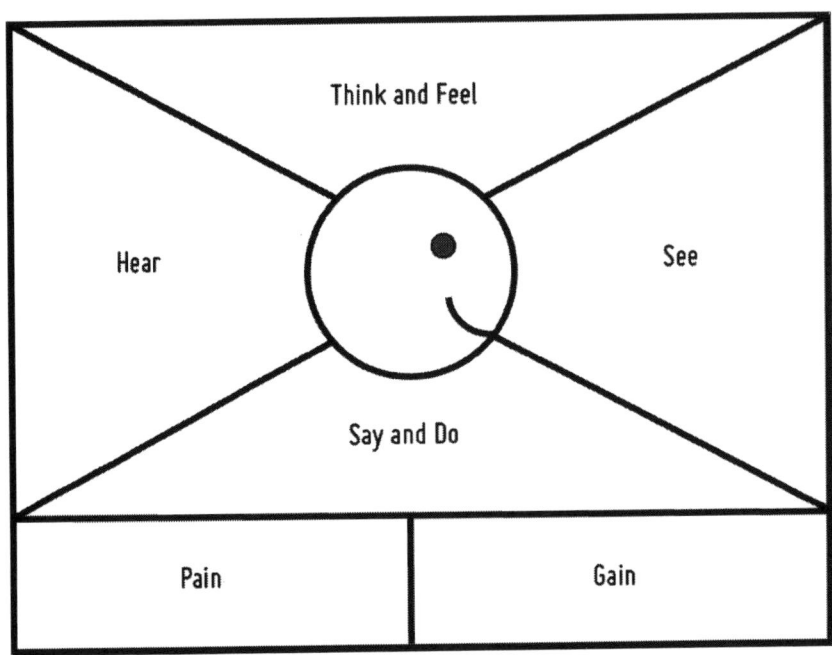

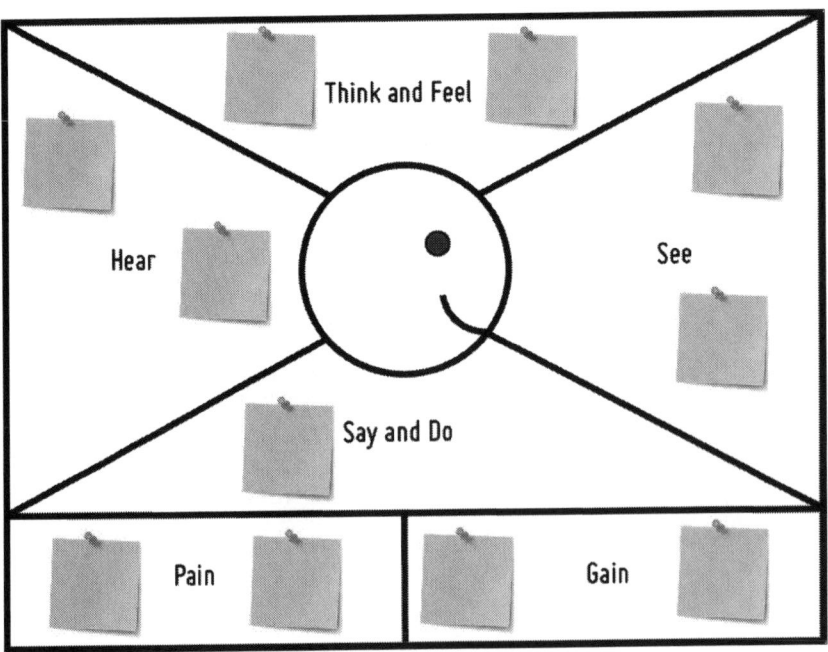

empathy map

WHAT IS IT?

Empathy Map is a tool that helps the design team empathize with people they are designing for, You can create an empathy map for a group of customers or a persona.

WHO INVENTED IT?

Scott Matthews and Dave Gray at PLANE now Dachis Group.

WHY USE THIS METHOD?

This tool helps a design team understand the customers and their context.

CHALLENGES

1. Emotions must be inferred by observing clues.
2. This method does not provide the same level of rigor as traditional personas but requires less investment.

WHEN TO USE THIS METHOD

1. Know Context
2. Know User
3. Frame insights

RESOURCES

1. Empathy map template
2. White board
3. Dry-erase markers
4. Post-it-notes
5. Pens
6. Video Camera

HOW TO USE THIS METHOD

1. A team of 3 to 10 people is a good number for this method.
2. This method can be used with personas.
3. Draw a cirle to represent your target persona.
4. Divide the circle into sections that represent aspects of that person's sensory experience.
5. Ask your team to describe from the persona's point of view their experience.
6. What are the persona's needs and desires?
7. Populate the map by taking note of the following traits of your user as you review your notes, audio, and video from your fieldwork: What are they thinking, feeling, saying, doing, hearing, seeing?
8. Fill in the diagram with real, tangible, sensory experiences.
9. 20 minutes to one hour is a good duration for this exercise.
10. Ask another group of people to look at your map and suggest improvements or refinements.

REFERENCES

1. Gray, Dave; Brown, Sunni; Macanufo, James (2010). Gamestorming: A Playbook for Innovators, Rulebreakers, and Changemakers. O'Reilly Media, Inc

innovation diagnostic

WHAT IS IT?

An innovation diagnostic is an evaluation of an organization's innovation capabilities. It reviews practices by stakeholders which may help or hinder innovation. An innovation diagnostic is the first step in preparing an implementing a strategy to create an organizational culture that supports innovation.

WHY USE THIS METHOD?

1. It helps organizations develop sustainable competitive advantage.
2. Helps identify innovation opportunities
3. Helps develop innovation strategy.

WHEN TO USE THIS METHOD

1. Know Context
2. Know User
3. Frame insights
4. Explore Concepts
5. Make Plans

HOW TO USE THIS METHOD

An innovation diagnostic reviews organizational and stakeholder practices using both qualitative and quantitative methods including

1. The design and development process
2. Strategic practices and planning.
3. The ability of an organization to monitor and respond to relevant trends.
4. Technologies
5. Organizational flexibility
6. Ability to innovate repeatedly and consistently

interview: contextual inquiry

WHAT IS IT?

Contextual inquiry involves one-on-one observations and interviews of activities in the context. Contextual inquiry has four guiding principles:

1. Context
2. Partnership with users.
3. Interpretation
4. Focus on particular goals.

WHO INVENTED IT?

Whiteside, Bennet, and Holtzblatt 1988

WHY USE THIS METHOD?

1. Contextual interviews uncover tacit knowledge about people's context.
2. The information gathered can be detailed.
3. The information produced by contextual inquiry is relatively reliable

CHALLENGES

1. End users may not have the answers
2. Contextual inquiry may be difficult to challenge even if it is misleading.

SEE ALSO

1. Questionnaire
2. Interview
3. Affinity diagram
4. Scenario
5. Persona
6. Ethnography
7. Contextual design

WHEN TO USE THIS METHOD

1. Know Context
2. Know User
3. Frame insights

HOW TO USE THIS METHOD

1. Contextual inquiry may be structured as 2 hour one on one interviews.
2. The researcher does not usually impose tasks on the user.
3. Go to the user's context. Talk, watch listen and observe.
4. Understand likes and dislikes.
5. Collect stories and insights.
6. See the world from the user's point of view.
7. Take permission to conduct interviews.
8. Do one-on-one interviews.
9. The researcher listens to the user.
10. 2 to 3 researchers conduct an interview.
11. Understand relationship between people, product and context.
12. Document with video, audio and notes.

REFERENCES

1. Beyer, H. and Holtzblatt, K., Contextual Design: Defining Customer-Centered Systems, Morgan Kaufmann Publishers Inc., San Francisco (1997).
2. Wixon and J. Ramey (Eds.), Field Methods Case Book for Product Design. John Wiley & Sons, Inc., NY, NY, 1996.

Photo: photocase.com – AlexAlex

interview: extreme user

WHAT IS IT?
Interview experienced or inexperienced users of a product or service. in order to discover useful insights that can be applied to the general users.

WHY USE THIS METHOD?
Extreme user's solutions to problems can inspire solutions for general users. Their behavior can be more exaggerated than general users so it is sometimes easier to develop useful insights from these groups.

CHALLENGES
1. Keep control
2. Be prepared
3. Be aware of bias
4. Be neutral
5. Select location carefully

WHEN TO USE THIS METHOD
1. Know Context
2. Know User
3. Frame insights
4. Explore Concepts

HOW TO USE THIS METHOD
1. Do a timeline of your activity and break it into main activities
2. Identify very experienced or very inexperienced users of a product or service in an activity area.
3. Explore their experiences through interview.
4. Discover insights that can inspire design.
5. Refine design based on insights.

RESOURCES
1. Computer
2. Notebook
3. Pens
4. Video camera
5. Release forms
6. Interview plan or structure
7. Questions, tasks and discussion items
8. Confidentiality agreement

REFERENCES
1. Rubin, Herbert and Irene Rubin. Qualitative Interviewing: The Art of Hearing Data. 2nd edition. Thousand Oaks, CA: Sage Publications, 2004. Print.
2. Kvale, Steinar. Interviews: An Introduction to Qualitative Research Interviewing, Sage Publications, 1996
3. Foddy, William. Constructing Questions for Interviews, Cambridge University Press, 1993

Photo: photocase.com – gregpeppers

A1 A2 A3 B1 B2 B3 C1 C2 C3
A4 **A** A5 B4 **B** B5 C4 **C** C5
A6 A7 A8 B6 B7 B8 C6 C7 C8

D1 D2 D3 **A** **B** **C** E1 E2 E3
D4 **D** D5 **D** ■ **E** E4 **E** E5
D6 D7 D8 **F** **G** **H** E6 E7 E8

F1 F2 F3 G1 G2 G3 H1 H2 H3
F4 **F** F5 G4 **G** G5 H4 **H** H5
F6 F7 F8 G6 G7 G8 H6 H7 H8

74

lotus blossom

WHAT IS IT?

The lotus blossom is a creativity technique that consists a framework for idea generation that starts by generating eight concept themes based on a central theme. Each concept then serves as the basis for eight further theme explorations or variations.

WHO INVENTED IT?

Yasuo Matsumura, Director of the Clover Management Research

WHY USE THIS METHOD?

1. There is a hierarchy of ideas
2. This method requires that a quantity of ideas is generated.
3. shifts you from reacting to a static snapshot of the problem and broadens your perspective toward the problem and the relationships and connections between its components

CHALLENGES

1. It is a somewhat rigid model. Not every problem will require the same number of concepts to be developed.

WHEN TO USE THIS METHOD

1. Explore Concepts

HOW TO USE THIS METHOD

1. Draw up a lotus blossom diagram made up of a square in the center of the diagram and eight circles surrounding the square;
2. Write the problem in the center box of the diagram.
3. Write eight related ideas around the center.
4. Each idea then becomes the central idea of a new theme or blossom.
5. Follow step 3 with all central ideas.

RESOURCES

1. Paper
2. Pens
3. White board
4. Dry-erase markers
5. Post-it-notes.

REFERENCES

1. Michalko M., Thinkpak, Berkeley, California, Ten Speed Press, 1994.
2. Michalko, Michael, Thinkertoys: A handbook of creative-thinking techniques, Second Edition, Ten Speed Press, 2006, Toronto;
3. Sloane, Paul. The Leader's Guide to Lateral Thinking Skills: Unlocking the Creativity and Innovation in You and Your Team (Paperback - 3 Sep 2006);

low fidelity prototyping

WHAT IS IT?

Cardboard prototyping is a quick and cheap way of gaining insight and informing decision making without the need for costly invest-ment. Simulates function but not aesthetics of proposed design. Prototypes help compare alternatives and help answer questions about interactions or experiences.

WHY USE THIS METHOD?

1. May provide the proof of concept
2. It is physical and visible
3. Inexpensive and fast.
4. Useful for refining functional and percep-tual interactions.
5. Assists to identify any problems with the design.
6. Helps to reduce the risks
7. Helps members of team to be in alignment on an idea.
8. Helps make abstract ideas concrete.
9. Feedback can be gained from the user

CHALLENGES

1. Producer might get too attached to pro-totype and it becomes jewelry because it is beautiful rather than a design tool.

WHEN TO USE THIS METHOD

1. Know Context
2. Know User
3. Frame insights
4. Explore Concepts

Image Copyright Liudmila P. Sundikova, 2012
Used under license from Shutterstock.com

HOW TO USE THIS METHOD

1. Construct models, not illustrations
2. Select the important tasks, interactions or experiences to be prototyped.
3. Build to understand problems.
4. If it is beautiful you have invested too much.
5. Make it simple
6. Assemble a kit of inexpensive materials
7. Preparing for a test
8. Select users
9. Conduct test
10. Record notes on the 8x5 cards.
11. Evaluate the results
12. Iterate

RESOURCES

1. Paper
2. Cardboard
3. Wire
4. Foam board,
5. Post-it-notes
6. Hot melt glue

REFERENCES

1. Sefelin, R., Tscheligi, M., & Gukker, V. (2003). Paper Prototyping — What is it good for? A Comparison of paper — and Computer — based Low fidelity Prototyping, CHI 2003, 778-779
2. Snyder, Carolyn (2003). Paper Prototyping: the fast and easy way to design and refine user interfaces. San Francisco, CA: Morgan Kaufmann

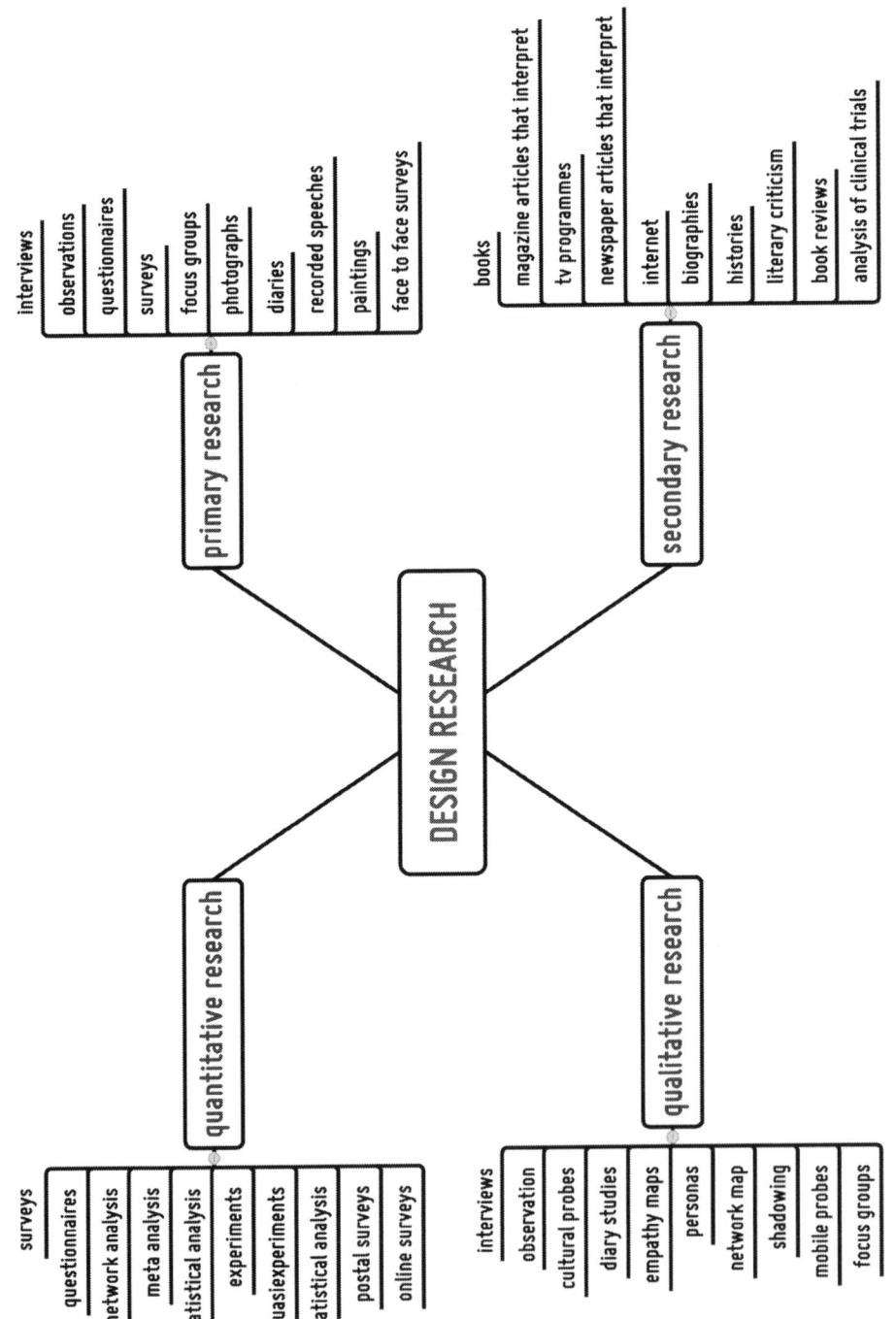

DESIGN RESEARCH

primary research
- interviews
- observations
- questionnaires
- surveys
- focus groups
- photographs
- diaries
- recorded speeches
- paintings
- face to face surveys

secondary research
- books
- magazine articles that interpret
- tv programmes
- newspaper articles that interpret
- internet
- biographies
- histories
- literary criticism
- book reviews
- analysis of clinical trials

quantitative research
- surveys
- questionnaires
- network analysis
- meta analysis
- atistical analysis
- experiments
- uasiexperiments
- atistical analysis
- postal surveys
- online surveys

qualitative research
- interviews
- observation
- cultural probes
- diary studies
- empathy maps
- personas
- network map
- shadowing
- mobile probes
- focus groups

mind map

WHAT IS IT?
A mind map is a diagram used to represent the affinities or connections between a number of ideas or things. Understanding connections is the starting point for design. Mind maps are a method of analyzing information and relationships.

WHO INVENTED IT?
Porphry of Tyros 3rd century BC.
Allan Collins, Northwestern University 1960, USA

WHY USE THIS METHOD?
1. The method helps identify relationships.
2. There is no right or wrong with mind maps. They help with they help with memory and organization.
3. Problem solving and brainstorming
4. Relationship discovery
5. Summarizing information
6. Memorizing information

CHALLENGES
Print words clearly, use color and images for visual impact.

WHEN TO USE THIS METHOD
7. Know Context
8. Know User
9. Frame insights
10. Explore Concepts
11. Make Plans

HOW TO USE THIS METHOD
1. Start in the center with a key word or idea. Put box around this node.
2. Use images, symbols, or words for nodes.
3. Select key words.
4. Keep the key word names of nodes s simple and short as possible.
5. Associated nodes should be connected with lines to show affinities.
6. Make the lines the same length as the word/image they support.
7. Use emphasis such as thicker lines to show the strength of associations in your mind map.
8. Use radial arrangement of nodes.

RESOURCES
1. Paper
2. Pens
3. White board
4. Dry-erase markers

REFERENCES
1. Mind maps as active learning tools', by Willis, CL. Journal of computing sciences in colleges. ISSN: 1937-4771. 2006. Volume: 21 Issue: 4
2. Mind Maps as Classroom Exercises John W. Budd The Journal of Economic Education, Vol. 35, No. 1 (Winter, 2004), pp. 35-46 Published by: Taylor & Francis, Ltd.

misuse scenario

WHAT IS IT?
This is a method that focuses on possible misuse, both unintentional and malicious, of a product or service. The method involves use of scenarios and personas to envision possible misuse cases. These may be:
1. Typical scenarios
2. Atypical scenarios
3. Extreme scenarios

WHO INVENTED IT?
Ian Alexander 2003

WHY USE THIS METHOD?
1. Considering misuse reduces the possibility that a product will fail in use.
2. Consider on projects where there is potential for misuse.
3. High volume manufactured products have high potential for misuse.

CHALLENGES
1. Use customer service feedback to construct misuse scenarios.
2. It is sometimes hard to envision misuse scenarios for new products.

WHEN TO USE THIS METHOD
1. Know Context
2. Know User
3. Frame insights
4. Explore Concepts

HOW TO USE THIS METHOD
1. Think of various types of scenarios and when they may become misuse scenarios.
2. Talk to experts and ask them to provide scenarios of misuse.
3. Consider the context of use and how that may influence misuse.
4. Brainstorm with team to create scenarios of misuse.
5. Create a list of misuse scenarios.
6. Brainstorm remedies for misuse and modify design to remedy misuse.

RESOURCES
1. Pen
2. Paper
3. White board
4. Dry-erase markers
5. Camera

REFERENCES
1. Alexander, Ian, Use/Misuse Case Analysis Elicits Non-Functional Requirements, Computing & Control Engineering Journal, Vol 14, 1, pp 40-45, February 2003
2. Sindre, Guttorm and Andreas L. Opdahl, Templates for Misuse Case Description, Proc. 7th Intl Workshop on Requirements Engineering, Foundation for Software Quality (REFSQ'2001), Interlaken, Switzerland, 4-5 June 2001

Photo: photocase.com – kallejipp

mobile diary study

WHAT IS IT?

A mobile diary studies is a method that uses portable devices to capture a person's experiences in context when and where they happen such as their work place or home. Participants can create diary entries from their location on mobile phones or tablets.

WHY USE THIS METHOD?

1. Most people carry a mobile phone.
2. It is a convenient method of recording diary entries.
3. It is easier to collect the data than collecting written diaries.
4. Collection of data happens in real time.
5. Mobile devices have camera, voice and written capability.

CHALLENGES

1. Can miss non verbal feedback.
2. Technology may be unreliable

WHEN TO USE THIS METHOD

1. Know Context
2. Know User
3. Frame insights

HOW TO USE THIS METHOD

1. Define intent
2. Define audience
3. Define context
4. Define technology
5. Automated text messages are sent to participants to prompt an entry.
6. Analyze data

RESOURCES

1. Smart phones,
2. Cameras,
3. Laptops and
4. Tablets

REFERENCES

Coover, R. (2004) 'Using Digital Media Tools and Cross-Cultural Research,Analysis and Representation', Visual Studies19(1): 6—25.
Dicks, B., B. Mason, A. Coffey and P. Atkinson (2005) Qualitative Research and Hypermedia: Ethnography for the Digital Age. London: SAGE.
Kozinets R.V. (2010a), Netnography. Doing Ethnographic Research Online, Sage, London.

image: © Adamr | Dreamstime.com

objectives tree

WHAT IS IT?

Objective Tree method, also known as decision tree, is a tool for clarifying the goals of a project.

The objective tree method shows a structured hierarchy of goals with higher level goals branching into related groups of sub goals.

WHY USE THIS METHOD?

1. An objectives tree is a visual way of mapping your design objectives so that you can discuss and refine them.
2. Building a better understanding of the project objectives.
3. It is a way to refine vague goals into more concrete and achievable goals.
4. Build stakeholder consensus.
5. Identify potential constraints

CHALLENGES

1. Consider the likely stakeholders and constraints.
2. Be precise

SEE ALSO

1. Decision tree
2. Concept tree
3. Problem tree

WHEN TO USE THIS METHOD

1. Define intent

HOW TO USE THIS METHOD

1. Prepare a list of design objectives. This can be done by brainstorming within your team and by undertaking research of your customers, their needs and desires. You can create an objective tree from a problem tree. Convert each problem into an objective.
2. Create a written list of objectives.
3. Create lists of higher and lower level objectives by sorting your original list of objectives. This can be done with an affinity diagram.
4. Create an objectives tree, showing hierarchical relationships and interconnections
5. Place each task in a box.
6. Connect the boxes with lines show associations.
7. Iterate.
8. Make the task descriptions as simple as possible

RESOURCES

1. White board
2. Dry-erase markers.

REFERENCES

1. ODI (2009): Problem Tree Analysis. Successful Communication: Planning Tools. London: ODI
2. Campbell, K.l.i.; Garforth, C.; Heffernan, C.; Morton, J.; Paterson, R.; Rymer, C. ; Upton, M. (2006): The Problem Tree. Analysis of the causes and effects of problems. The Problem Tree. Analysis of the causes and effects of problems.

observation

WHAT IS IT?

This method involves observing people in their natural activities and usual context such as work environment. With direct observation the researcher is present and indirect observation the activities may be recorded by means such as video or digital voice recording.

WHY USE THIS METHOD?

1. Allows the observer to view what users actually do in context.
2. Indirect observation uncovers activity that may have previously gone unnoticed

CHALLENGES

1. Observation does not explain the cause of behavior.
2. Obtrusive observation may cause participants to alter their behavior.
3. Analysis can be time consuming.
4. Observer bias can cause the researcher to look only where they think they will see useful information.

WHEN TO USE THIS METHOD

1. Know Context
2. Know User
3. Frame insights

HOW TO USE THIS METHOD

1. Define objectives
2. Define participants and obtain their cooperation.
3. Define The context of the observation: time and place.
4. In some countries the law requires that you obtain written consent to video people.
5. Define the method of observation and the method of recording information. Common methods are taking written notes, video or audio recording.
6. Run a test session.
7. Hypothesize an explanation for the phenomenon
8. Predict a logical consequence of the hypothesis
9. Test your hypothesis by observation
10. Analyze the data gathered and create a list of insights derived from the observations.

RESOURCES

1. Note pad
2. Pens
3. Camera
4. Video camera
5. Digital voice recorder

REFERENCES

1. Kosso, Peter (2011). A Summary of Scientific Method. Springer. pp. 9. ISBN 9400716133,

PERSONA

PERSONA NAME
....

DEMOGRAPHICS
....
....
....
....

CHARACTERISTIC STATEMENT
....
....
....
....
....

GOALS
....
....
....
....

AMBITIONS
....
....
....
....

INFLUENCERS AND ACTIVITIES
....
....
....
....

SCENARIOS
....
....
....
....

OTHER CHARACTERISTICS

TYPE: TYPE: TYPE: TYPE: TYPE: TYPE: TYPE: TYPE: TYPE:

personas

WHAT IS IT?

"A persona is a archetypal character that is meant to represent a group of users in a role who share common goals, attitudes and behaviors when interacting with a particular product or service Personas are user models that are presented as specific individual humans. They are not actual people, but are synthesized directly from observations of real people."(Cooper)

WHO INVENTED IT?

Alan Cooper 1998

WHY USE THIS METHOD?

1. Helps create empathy for users and reduces self reference.
2. Use as tool to analyze and gain insight into users.
3. Help in gaining buy-in from stake holders.

CHALLENGES

1. Portigal (2008) has claimed that personas give a "cloak of smug customer-centricity" while actually distancing a team from engagement with real users and their needs

REFERENCES

1. Pruitt, John & Adlin, Tamara. The Persona Lifecycle : Keeping People in Mind Throughout Product Design. Morgan Kaufmann, 2006. ISBN 0-12-566251-3

WHEN TO USE THIS METHOD

1. Know Context
2. Know User
3. Frame insights
4. Explore Concept

HOW TO USE THIS METHOD

1. Inaccurate personas can lead to a false understandings of the end users. Personas need to be created using data from real users.
2. Collect data through observation, interviews, ethnography.
3. Segment the users or customers
4. Create the Personas
5. Avoid Stereotypes
6. Each persona should be different. Avoid fringe characteristics. Personas should each have three to four life goals which are personal aspirations,
7. Personas are given a name, and photograph.
8. Design personas can be followed by building customer journeys

RESOURCES

1. Raw data on users from interviews or other research
2. Images of people similar to segmented customers.
3. Computer
4. Graphics software

dark horse prototype

WHAT IS IT?

A dark horse prototype is your most creative idea built as a fast prototype. The innovative approach serves as a focus for finding the optimum real solution to the design problem.

WHO INVENTED IT?

One of the methods taught at Stanford University.

WHY USE THIS METHOD?

1. This method is a way of breaking free of average solutions and exploring unknown territory
2. A way of challenging assumptions.

CHALLENGES

1. Fear of unexplored directions
2. Fear of change
1. Designers can become too attached to their prototypes and allow them to become jewelry that stands in the way of further refinement.
2. Client may believe that system is real.

WHEN TO USE THIS METHOD

1. Explore Concepts

HOW TO USE THIS METHOD

1. After initial brainstorming sessions select with your team the most challenging, interestingly or thought provoking idea.
2. Create a low resolution prototype of the selected idea.
3. With your team analyze and discuss the prototype.
4. Brainstorm ways of bringing back the dark horse concept into a realizable solution.

REFERENCES

1. Constantine, L. L., Windl, H., Noble, J., and Lockwood, L. A. D. "From Abstraction to Realization in User Interface Design: Abstract Prototypes Based on Canonical Components." Working Paper, The Convergence Colloquy, July 2000.

pictive

1. WHAT IS IT?

PICTIVE (Plastic Interface for Collaborative Technology Initiative through Video Exploration) is a low fidelity participatory design method used to develop graphical user interfaces. It allows users to participate in the development process. A PICTIVE prototype gives a user a sense of what a system or a piece of software will look like and how it will behave when completed.

WHO INVENTED IT?

Developed by Michael J. Muller and others at Bell Communications Research around 1990

WHY USE THIS METHOD?

2. Less development time.
3. Less development costs.
4. Involves users.
5. Gives quantifiable user feedback.
6. Facilitates system implementation since users know what to expect.
7. Results user oriented solutions.
8. Gets users with diverse experience involved.

CHALLENGES

1. Designers can become too attached to their prototypes and allow them to become jewelry that stands in the way of further refinement.
2. Don't worry about it being pretty.

WHEN TO USE THIS METHOD

1. Explore Concepts

HOW TO USE THIS METHOD

1. A PICTIVE is usually made from simple available tools and materials like pens, paper, Post-It stickers, paper clips and icons on cards.
2. Allow thirty minutes for initial design.
3. Allow ten minutes for user testing.
4. Ten minutes for modification.
5. Five minutes for user testing.
6. Create task scenario.
7. Anything that moves or changes should be a separate element.
8. The designer uses these materials to represent elements such as drop-down boxes, menu bars, and special icons. During a design session, users modify the mock up based on their own experience.
9. Take notes for later review.
10. Record the session with a video camera
11. The team then reviews the ideas and develops a strategy to apply them.
12. A PICTIVE enables non technical people to participate in the design process.

REFERENCES

1. Michael J. Muller PICTIVE an exploration in participatory design. Published in: · Proceeding CHI '91 Proceedings of the SIGCHI Conference on Human Factors in Computing Systems Pages 225-231 ACM New York, NY, USA ©1991 table of contents ISBN:0-89791-383-3 doi 10.1145/108844.108896

rich pictures

WHAT IS IT?

Rich Pictures is a method for learning about complex or ill-defined problems by asking participants to draw detailed pictures of them and to explain the drawings.

WHO INVENTED IT?

Rich pictures originated in Soft Systems Methodologies developed during the 1960s and 1970s by Peter Checkland and students at Lancaster University

WHY USE THIS METHOD?

1. This is a method for assisting in empathy which is an important factor in gaining acceptance and creating successful design.

REFERENCES

1. Monk, A. F. Lightweight techniques to encourage innovative user interface design. In L. Wood & R. Zeno, eds., Bridging the Gap: Transforming User Requirements into User Interface Design. CRC Press,Boca Raton, 1997.
2. Avison, D. and Fitzgerald, G. Information Systems Development: Methodologies, Techniques and Tools. Blackwell Scientific Publishers, Oxford,1988.

WHEN TO USE THIS METHOD

1. Know Context
2. Know User
3. Frame insights

HOW TO USE THIS METHOD

1. The moderator asks each participant to draw two pictures.
2. Ask the participants to draw a picture of how they want to see a situation, activity, product, service or experience in the future.
3. Ask the participants to draw a second picture of how they see the current situation, activity, product, service or experience.
4. Each participant explains first the picture of the present situation;
5. Ask the participants to explain what, when, where, how and why for each picture.
6. Brainstorm ideas to move from the present to the future.

RESOURCES

1. Pens
2. Paper
3. Digital voice recorder
4. Camera
5. Video camera.

scenarios

WHAT IS IT?

A scenario is a narrative or story about how people may experience a design in a particular future context of use. They can be used to predict or explore future interactions with concept products or services. Scenarios can be presented by media such as storyboards or video or be written. They can feature single or multiple actors participating in product or service interactions.

WHO INVENTED IT?

Herman Kahn, Rand Corporation 1950, USA

WHY USE THIS METHOD?

1. Scenarios become a focus for discussion which helps evaluate and refine concepts.
2. Usability issues can be explored at a very early stage in the design process.
3. The are useful tool to align a team vision.
4. Scenarios help us create an end to end experience.
5. Interactive experiences involve the dimension of time.
6. Personas give us a framework to evaluate possible solutions.

CHALLENGES

1. Generate scenarios for a range of situations.
2. Include problem situations
3. Hard to envision misuse scenarios.

WHEN TO USE THIS METHOD

1. Frame insights
2. Generate Concepts
3. Create Solutions

HOW TO USE THIS METHOD

1. Identify the question to investigate.
2. Decide time and scope for the scenario process.
3. Identify stake holders and uncertainties.
4. Define the scenarios.
5. Create storyboards of users goals, activities, motivations and tasks.
6. Act out the scenarios.
7. The session can be videotaped.
8. Analyze the scenarios through discussion.
9. Summarize insights

RESOURCES

1. Storyboard templates
2. Pens
3. Video cameras
4. Props
5. White board
6. Dry-erase markers

REFERENCES

1. "Scenarios," IDEO Method Cards. ISBN 0-9544132-1-0
2. Carroll, John M. Making Use: Scenario-based design of human-computer interactions. MIT Press, 2000.
3. Carroll J. M. Five Reasons for Scenario Based Design. Elsevier Science B. V. 2000.
4. Carroll, John M. Scenario-Based Design: Envisioning Work and Technology in System Development.

shadowing

WHAT IS IT?

Shadowing is observing people in context. The researcher accompanies the user and observes user experiences and activities. It allows the researcher and designer to develop design insights through observation and shared experiences with users.

WHO INVENTED IT?

Alex Bavelas 1944
Lucy Vernile, Robert A. Monteiro 1991

WHY USE THIS METHOD?

1. This method can help determine the difference between what subjects say they do and what they really do.
2. It helps in understanding the point of view of people. Successful design results from knowing the users.
3. Define intent
4. Can be used to evaluate concepts.

CHALLENGES

1. Selecting the wrong people to shadow.
2. Hawthorne Effect, The observer can influence the daily activities under being studied.

WHEN TO USE THIS METHOD

1. Know Context
2. Know User
3. Frame insights
4. Generate Concepts

HOW TO USE THIS METHOD

1. Prepare
2. Select carefully who to shadow.
3. Observe people in context by members of your design team.
4. Capture behaviors that relate to product function.
5. Identify issues and user needs.
6. Create design solutions based on observed and experienced user needs.
7. Typical periods can be one day to one week.

RESOURCES

1. Video camera
2. Digital still camera
3. Note pad
4. Laptop Computer

SEE ALSO

1. Day in the life
2. Fly on the wall

REFERENCES

1. McDonald, Seonaidh. "Studying Actions in Context: A Qualitative Shadowing Method for Organizational Research." Qualitative Research. The Robert Gordon University. SAGE Publications. London. 2005. p455-473.
2. Alan Bryman, Emma Bell. Business Research Meythods. Oxford University Press 2007 ISBN 978-0-19-928498-6

image: © Vwimage | Dreamstime.com

sociodrama

WHAT IS IT?

Sociodrama is concerned with social learning and problem solving in a group by dramatic methods. Actors play out everyday experiences and interact with an audience. The method is used in institutions such as police academies for training.

WHO INVENTED IT?

Jacob L. Moreno 1910

WHY USE THIS METHOD?

1. Used in business, education, and professional training

WHEN TO USE THIS METHOD

1. Know Context
2. Know User
3. Explore Concepts

REFERENCES

1. Kellermann, P. (2007) Sociodrama and Collective Trauma.
2. B. Clark, J. Burmeister, and M. Maciel, "Psychodrama: Advances in Theory and Practice." (2007) Taylor and Frances: USA. ISBN 0-415-41914-X
3. The workbook. A guide to the development and presentation of issue oriented, audience interactive, improvisational theatre. New York: Taylor & Francis Group. Dayton, T. (1990). Drama games. Techniques for self development.

HOW TO USE THIS METHOD

1. The actors are briefed in their roles, and characters motivations, expected behavior in the scene.
2. The activity may take place on a stage.
3. A common approach is to use a volunteer chosen from the of participants being trained who is given a role to perform.
4. The moderator will ask the actor to stop and then ask the audience for critical feedback of the scene. This method relies on dialogue with the audience. The dialogue should occur in a neutral manner.
5. The moderator steers the dialogue which is the tool for education and conscience raising.

RESOURCES

1. Stage or theater
2. Props
3. Costumes
4. Video camera

synectics

WHAT IS IT?

Synectics is a structured creativity method that is based on analogy. Synectics is based on observations collected during thousands of hours of group process and group problem solving and decision making activities (Nolan 1989)The word synectics combines derives from Greek "the bringing together of diverse elements."

WHO INVENTED IT?

George Prince and William Gordon 1976

WHY USE THIS METHOD?

1. Use to stimulate creative thinking and generate new problem solving approaches.
2. Synectics provides an environment in which risk taking is validated.
3. Synectics can be fun and productive.

CHALLENGES

1. Synectics is more demanding than brainstorming,
2. If the analogy is too obvious, then it may not promote innovative thinking.
3. Synectics works best as a group process.

WHEN TO USE THIS METHOD

1. Frame insights
2. Generate Concepts

HOW TO USE THIS METHOD

1. Problem definition.
2. Create an analogy. Use ideas from the natural or man-made world, connections with historical events, your location, etc.
3. Use this Sentence Stem: An is a lot like a y because...
4. Use a syntectic trigger Mechanism like a picture, poem, song, drawing etc. to start your analogical reasoning.
5. The group generates as many solution approaches, called springboards, as possible.
6. Idea selection.
7. Excursions – Structured side trips.
8. Develop the selected ideas into concepts.
9. Analyze the connections in the analogy you have created.

RESOURCES

1. Paper
2. Pens
3. White board
4. Dry-erase markers

REFERENCES

1. Gordon, William J.J. Synectics: The Development of Creative Capacity. (New York: Harper and row, Publishers, 1961
2. Nolan, Vincent. "Whatever Happened to Synectics?" Creativity and Innovation Management, v. 21 n.1 (2003): 25.

STORYBOARD

PROJECT

NAME

DATE

PAGE

DIALOGUE

ACTION

DIALOGUE

ACTION

DIALOGUE

ACTION

storyboards

WHAT IS IT?

The storyboard is a narrative tool derived from cinema. A storyboard is a form of prototyping which communicates each step of an activity, experience or interaction. Used in films and multimedia as well as product and UX design. Storyboards consists of a number of 'frames' that communicate a sequence of events in context.

WHO INVENTED IT?

Invented by Walt Disney in 1927. Disney credited animator Webb Smith with creating the first storyboard. By 1937-38 all studios were using storyboards.

WHY USE THIS METHOD?

1. Can help gain insightful user feedback.
2. Conveys an experience.
3. Can use a storyboard to communicate a complex task as a series of steps.
4. Allows the proposed activities to be discussed and refined.
5. Storyboards can be used to help designers identify opportunities or use problems.

CHALLENGES

1. Interaction between the storyboard and a user is limited (Landay & Myers, 1996).
2. Participants may not be able to draw well.
3. There haven't been conclusive studies about the effectiveness of storyboards for some design activities.
4. Storyboarding is linear.
5. Not useful for detailed design.

WHEN TO USE THIS METHOD

1. Generate Concepts
2. Create Solutions

HOW TO USE THIS METHOD

1. Decide what story you want to describe.
2. Choose a story and a message: what do you want the storyboard to express?
3. Create your characters
4. Think about the whole story first rather than one panel at a time.
5. Create the drafts and refine them through an iterative process. Refine.
6. Illustrations can be sketches or photographs.
7. Consider: Visual elements, level of detail, text, experiences and emotions, number of frames, and flow of time.
8. Keep text short and informative.
9. 6 to 12 frames.
10. Tell your story efficiently and effectively.
11. Brainstorm your ideas.

RESOURCES

1. Pens
2. Digital camera
3. Storyboard templates
4. Comic books for inspiration

REFERENCES

1. Giuseppe Cristiano Storyboard Design Course: Principles, Practice, and Technique Barron's Educational Series (October 1, 2007) ISBN-10: 0764137328

storytelling

WHAT IS IT?

A powerful story can help ensure the success of a new product, service or experience. Storytelling can be an effective method of presenting a point of view. Research methods can uncover meaningful stories from end users that illustrate needs or desires. These stories can become the basis of new designs and be used to support design decisions. Research shows that our attitudes, fears, hopes, and values are strongly influenced by story. Stories can be an effective way of communicating complex ideas and inspiring people to change.

WHO INVENTED IT?

1. Storytelling is one of the most ancient forms of human communication.

WHY USE THIS METHOD?

1. The stories help to get buy-in from people throughout the design process and may be used to help sell a final design.
2. Real life stories are persuasive.
3. They are different to advertising because they are able to influence a design if uncovered from users during the early research phases and provide authenticity.

CHALLENGES

1. A story with too much jargon will lose an audience.
2. Not everyone has the ability to tell vivid stories.
3. Stories are not always generalizable.

Photos: photocase.com – lube

WHEN TO USE THIS METHOD

1. Define intent
2. Know Context
3. Know User
4. Frame insights
5. Explore Concepts
6. Make Plans
7. Deliver Offering

HOW TO USE THIS METHOD

Answer in your story: What, why, when, who, where, how?
An effective story:
1. Is honest
2. Is real
3. Builds trust
4. Transmits values
5. Shares a vision
6. Shares knowledge
7. Helps Collaboration
8. Must differentiate you.
9. Uses humor
10. Engages the audience
11. Pose a problem and offer a resolution
12. Use striking imagery
13. Fit the audience
14. The audience must be able to act on it.

REFERENCES

1. Peter Guber Tell to Win: Connect, Persuade, and Triumph with the Hidden Power of Story. Publisher: Crown Business; 1ST edition (March 1, 2011) ISBN-10: 0307587959 ISBN-13: 978-0307587954

swot analysis

WHAT IS IT?
SWOT Analysis is a useful technique for understanding your strengths and weaknesses, and for identifying both the opportunities open to you and the threats you face.

WHO INVENTED IT?
Albert Humphrey 1965 Stanford University

WHY USE THIS METHOD?
1. SWOT analysis can help you uncover opportunities that you can exploit.
2. You can analysis both your own organization, product or service as well as those of competitors.
3. Helps develop a strategy of differentiation.
4. It is inexpensive

CHALLENGES
1. Use only verifiable information.
2. Have system for implementation.

WHEN TO USE THIS METHOD
1. Define intent
2. Know Context
3. Know User
4. Frame insights

RESOURCES
1. Post-it-notes
2. SWOT template
3. Pens
4. White board
5. Video camera
6. Dry-erase markers

HOW TO USE THIS METHOD
1. Explain basic rules of brainstorming.
2. Ask questions related to the SWOT categories.
3. Record answers on a white board or video
4. Categorize ideas into groups
5. Consider when evaluating "What will the institution gain or lose?"

REFERENCES
1. Armstrong. M. A handbook of Human Resource Management Practice (10th edition) 2006, Kogan Page, London ISBN 0-7494-4631-5

SOME SAMPLE SWOT QUESTIONS

STRENGTHS
1. Advantages of proposition
2. Capabilities
3. Competitive advantages
4. Marketing – reach, distribution
5. Innovative aspects
6. Location and geographical
7. Price, value, quality?
8. Accreditation, certifications
9. Unique selling proposition
10. Human resources
11. Experience,
12. Assets
13. Return on investment
14. Processes, IT, communications
15. Cultural, attitudinal, behavioral
16. Management cover, succession

WEAKNESSES
1. Value of proposition
2. Things we cannot do.
3. Things we are not good at
4. Perceptions of brand
5. Financial
6. Own known vulnerabilities
7. Time scales, deadlines and pressures
8. Reliability of data, plan predictability
9. Morale, commitment, leadership
10. Accreditation,
11. Cash flow, start-up cash-drain
12. Continuity, supply chain robustness
13. Effects on core activities, distraction
14. Processes and systems
15. Management cover, succession

OPPORTUNITIES
1. Market developments
2. Competitors' vulnerabilities
3. New USP's
4. Tactics – surprise, major contracts
5. Business and product development
6. Information and research
7. Partnerships, agencies, distribution
8. Industrial trends
9. Technologies
10. Innovations
11. Global changes
12. Market opportunities
13. Specialized market niches
14. New exports or imports
15. Volumes, production, economies
16. Seasonal, weather, fashion influences

THREATS
1. Political effects
2. Legislative effects
3. Obstacles faced
4. Insurmountable weaknesses
5. Environmental effects
6. IT developments
7. Competitor intentions
8. Loss of key staff
9. Sustainable financial backing
10. Market demand
11. New technologies, services, ideas
12. Vital contracts and partners
13. Sustaining internal capabilities
14. Economy – home, abroad
15. Seasonality, weather effects

talk out loud protocol

WHAT IS IT?

Think aloud or thinking out loud protocols involve participants verbalizing their thoughts while performing a set of tasks. Users are asked to say whatever they are looking at, thinking, doing, and experiencing. A related method is the think-aloud protocol where subjects also explain their actions.

WHO INVENTED IT?

Clayton Lewis IBM 1993

WHY USE THIS METHOD?

1. Provides an understanding of the user's mental model and interaction with the product.
2. Enables observers to see first-hand the process of task completion
3. The terminology the user uses to express an idea or function the design or and documentation.
4. Allows testers to understand how the user approaches the system.

CHALLENGES

1. The design team needs to be composed of people with a variety of skills.

WHEN TO USE THIS METHOD

1. Know Context
2. Know User
3. Frame insights
4. Explore Concepts

HOW TO USE THIS METHOD

1. Identify users.
2. Choose representative tasks.
3. Create a mock-up or prototype.
4. Select participants.
5. Provide the test users with the system or prototype to be tested and tasks.
6. Brief participants.
7. Take notes of everything that users say, without attempting to interpret their actions and words.
8. Iterate
9. Videotape the tests, then analyze the videotapes.

RESOURCES

1. Computer
2. Video camera
3. Note pad
4. Pens

unfocus group

WHAT IS IT?

Unfocus groups is a qualitative research method in which interviewers hold group interviews where the subjects are selected based on diverse viewpoints and backgrounds The participants may not be users of the product or service.

WHO INVENTED IT?

Uses methods pioneered by Liz Sanders and the consulting firm IDEO circa 2001

WHY USE THIS METHOD?

1. Goal is to get diverse perspectives.

CHALLENGES

1. Participants are removed from their usual context.
2. Non target market group may not be able to effectively define a product or service for target group.

WHEN TO USE THIS METHOD

1. Define intent
2. Know Context
3. Know User
4. Frame insights
5. Explore Concepts
6. Make Plans

HOW TO USE THIS METHOD

1. Assemble a diverse group of participants. Choose Diverse Participants Who:
◦   Are not likely to use the product or service,
◦   Are highly motivated.
◦   Are extreme users of the product
◦   Have a tangential connection with the product
◦   Don't want the product.
2. Select a good moderator.
3. Prepare a screening questionnaire.
4. Decide incentives for participants.
5. Select facility.
6. Recruit participants.
7. Provide refreshments.
8. Prepare the space. Participants should sit around a large table.
9. Describe rules.
10. First question should encourage talking and participation.
11. Provide simple materials such as paper and ask the participants to create crude prototypes for discussion.
12. Ask participants to act out ideas.
13. Record the feedback for idea generation phase.
14. Follow discussion guide.
15. At end of focus group summarize key points.
16. Moderator collects forms and debriefs focus group.

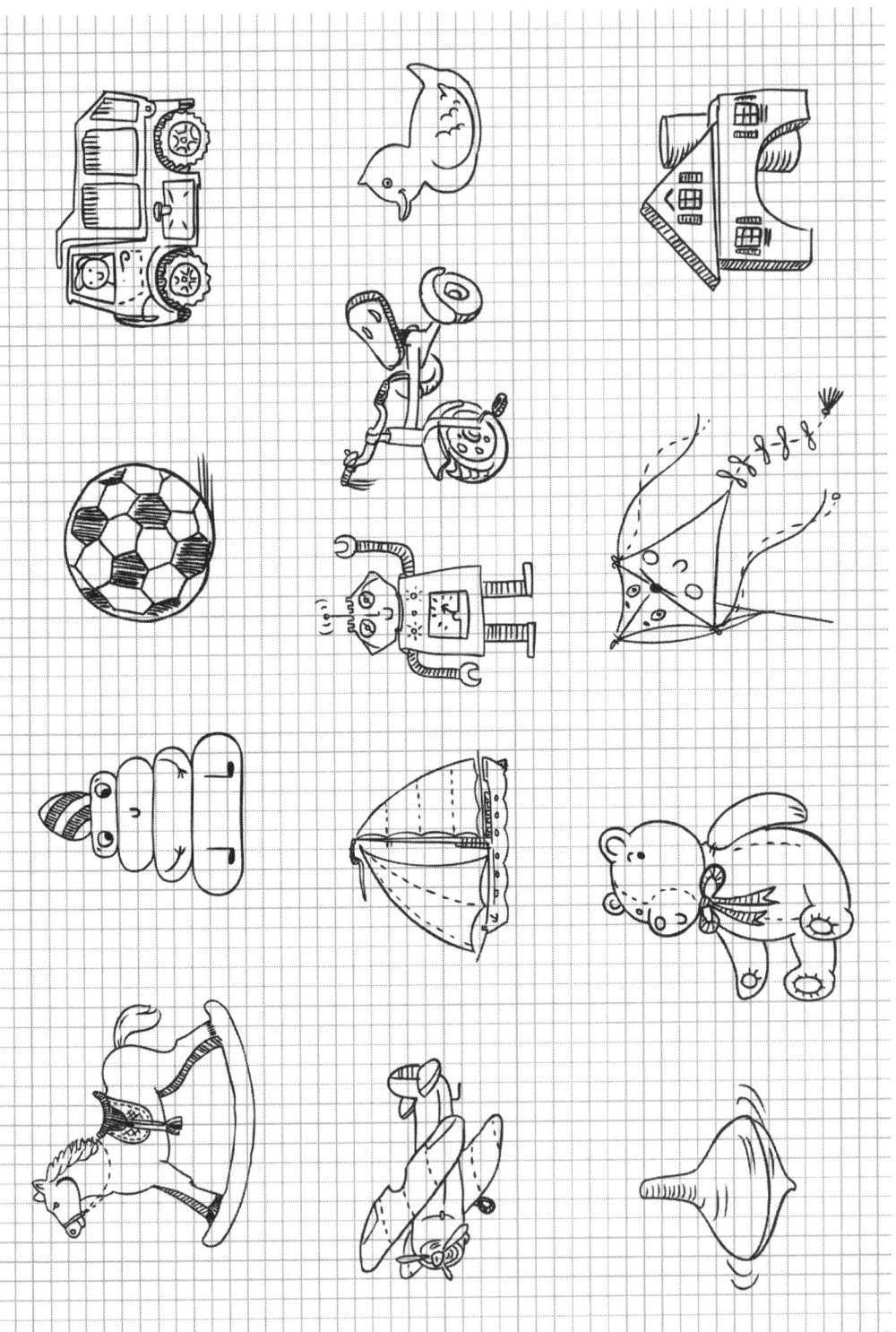

10 x 10 sketch method

WHAT IS IT?

This method is an approach to making early concept generation sketching more efficient in use of time than the method that stresses finished sketches early in the design process. It allows more time to explore ideas and so stresses the quality of thinking and the final solution. The 10 x 10 method involves creating ten rows with ten thumbnail sketches per row on each page.

WHY USE THIS METHOD?

1. It allows more exploration of alternative ideas in a shorter time
2. May lead to a final concept which is a better design than traditional approaches.
3. Prevents sketches from becoming jewelry in the mind of the designer and more important than the quality of the final design solution.

CHALLENGES

1. This method takes discipline

WHEN TO USE THIS METHOD

1. Explore Concepts

HOW TO USE THIS METHOD

1. Traditional design concept exploration involves a designer producing six to 12 alternative design concepts presented as attractive renderings
2. This method involves a designer making ten rows of ten simple fast cartoon like sketches per page.
3. Each sketch should be no larger than one inch by one inch.
4. The designer produces 5 to 20 pages of very fast sketches during first phase of concept exploration
5. Designs are reviewed and ranked by the design team following a discussion and presentation by the designer and a relatively small number are selected for iteration, recombination and further development.
6. At the next stage more finished and larger concept sketches are produced

RESOURCES

1. Paper
2. Fine line pens
3. Sharpie markers

index

index

other titles in the design methods series

Design Methods 1
200 ways to apply design thinking

Author: Robert A Curedale
Published by:
Design Community College Inc.
PO Box 1153
Topanga CA 90290 USA

Edition 1 November 2013

ISBN-10:0988236206
ISBN-13:978-0-9882362-0-2

Design Methods 2
200 more ways to apply design thinking

Author: Robert A Curedale
Published by:
Design Community College Inc.
PO Box 1153
Topanga CA 90290 USA

Edition 1 January 2013

ISBN-13: 978-0988236240
ISBN-10: 0988236249

The Design Thinking Manual

Author: Robert A Curedale
Published by:
Design Community College Inc.
PO Box 1153
Topanga CA 90290 USA

Edition 1 January 2013

ISBN-10: 0988236214
ISBN-13: 978-0-9882362-1-9

50 Brainstorming Methods

Author: Robert A Curedale
Published by:
Design Community College Inc.
PO Box 1153
Topanga CA 90290 USA

Edition 1 January 2013

ISBN-10: 0988236230
ISBN-13: 978-0-9882362-3-3

Structured Workshops

The author presents workshops online and in person in global locations for executives, engineers, designers, technology professionals and anyone interested in learning and applying these proven innovation methods. For information contact: info@curedale.com

about the author

Rob Curedale was born in Australia and worked as a designer, director and educator in leading design offices in London, Sydney, Switzerland, Portugal, Los Angeles, Silicon Valley, Detroit, and China. He designed and managed over 1,000 products and experiences as a consultant and in-house design leader for the world's most respected brands. Rob has three decades experience in every aspect of product development, leading design teams to achieve transformational improvements in operating and financial results. He has extensive experience in forging strategic growth, competitive advantage, and a background in expanding business into emerging markets through user advocacy and extensive cross cultural expertise. Rob's designs can be found in millions of homes and workplaces around the world.

Rob works currently as a Adjunct Professor at Art Center College of Design in Pasadena and consults to organizations in the United States and internationally and presents workshops related to design. He has taught as a member of staff and presented lectures and workshops at many respected design schools and universities throughout the world including Yale, Pepperdine University, Art Center Pasadena, Loyola University, Cranbrook, Pratt, Art Center Europe; a faculty member at SCA and UTS Sydney; as Chair of Product Design and Furniture Design at the College for Creative Studies in Detroit, then the largest product design school in North America, Art Institute Hollywood, Cal State San Jose, Escola De Artes e Design in Oporto Portugal, Instituto De Artes Visuals, Design e Marketing, Lisbon, Southern Yangtze University, Jiao Tong University in Shanghai and Nanjing Arts Institute in China.

Rob's design practice experience includes projects for HP, Philips, GEC, Nokia, Sun, Apple, Canon, Motorola, Nissan, Audi VW, Disney, RTKL, Governments of the UAE,UK, Australia, Steelcase, Hon, Castelli, Hamilton Medical, Zyliss, Belkin, Gensler, Haworth, Honeywell, NEC, Hoover, Packard Bell, Dell, Black & Decker, Coleman and Harmon Kardon. Categories including furniture, healthcare, consumer electronics, sporting, homewares, military, exhibits, packaging. His products and experiences can be found in millions of homes and businesses throughout the world.

Rob established and manages the largest network of designers and architects in the world with more than 300,000 professional members working in every field of design.

Made in the USA
Lexington, KY
27 July 2016